Using Yocto Project with BeagleBone Black

Unleash the power of the BeagleBone Black embedded platform with Yocto Project

H M Irfan Sadiq

[PACKT] PUBLISHING

BIRMINGHAM - MUMBAI

Using Yocto Project with BeagleBone Black

First published: June 2015

Production reference: 1250615

Published by Packt Publishing Ltd.
Livery Place
35 Livery Street
Birmingham B3 2PB, UK.

ISBN 978-1-78528-973-6

www.packtpub.com

Credits

Author
H M Irfan Sadiq

Reviewers
Daniel Garbanzo Hidalgo
Noor Ahsan Khawaja
Elango Palanisamy
Ankur Rameshchandra Tank
Mikhail Zakharov

Commissioning Editor
Amarabha Banerjee

Acquisition Editor
Sonali Vernekar

Content Development Editor
Mamata Walkar

Technical Editor
Edwin Moses

Copy Editors
Karuna Narayanan
Stuti Srivastava

Project Coordinator
Shipra Chawhan

Proofreader
Safis Editing

Indexer
Hemangini Bari

Production Coordinator
Nitesh Thakur

Cover Work
Nitesh Thakur

Foreword

From my embedded Linux testing experience, I have found working with embedded Linux to be very challenging. Multiple architectures, cross-compilation, and devices with different functionalities requiring different user space and kernel configurations are just a few examples. Yocto Project facilitates an embedded developer to overcome these challenges and many more. Instead of using Make and configure directly, BitBake lets you combine all the required steps, from fetching the code to installing in a recipe file, creating a layer of abstraction for the user.

Embedded Linux is everywhere these days, for example, set-top boxes, IPTVs, and in-flight infotainment systems. With the power of open source behind it, it can be GENIVI and Carrier Grade Linux, which are helping the vendors define standards to use Linux for different purposes.

Irfan has worked in OpenEmbedded and later on Yocto Project. With his keen interest in scripting and test automation, he has played an important role in the test automation project during his professional career. Working under my management, he has developed multiple solutions to solve testing-related problems for Yocto Project-based projects.

Yocto Project has some complex concepts and can be overwhelming for a new user. Most of the material available on Yocto Project caters to the advanced level concepts. This book, however, starts from the very basic concepts and slowly familiarizes the user with the advanced features provided.

It gives a comprehensive introduction to Yocto Project. By taking the example of BeagleBone, the low cost and already supported by Yocto Project evaluation board, Irfan takes you step by step, from setting up Yocto Project and building default images to moving on to advanced topics that cover how to create custom images. The book explains how you can utilize the existing applications and add your own applications to the filesystem. The final chapter(s) explains how to use the full power of Linux and Yocto Project and turn your inexpensive BeagleBone into any device of your choice, such as a home surveillance system, a gaming console, or a Wi-Fi hotspot.

If you are interested in developing an embedded solution using Linux, this book will provide you with a wealth of information. If you are already working on Yocto Project, this book will prove to be very helpful in understanding different concepts and utilizing the full power of Yocto Project.

Happy reading!

Khula Azmi
Engineering Manager QA at Mentor Graphics

About the Author

H M Irfan Sadiq was a Linux enthusiast as a graduate student. He started his career as an embedded system development engineer and has been working as an H.264 Decoder developer and optimizer for the VLIW architecture. He got an opportunity to work on multiple multimedia frameworks that are open source as well as proprietary. He tried to work in a start-up in the entirely different domain of web development. He has been working on OpenEmbedded and Yocto Project technologies since he joined Mentor Graphics as the technical lead back in 2010. He has been working on derivative technologies of Yocto Project and OpenEmbedded for quite some time now, spanning more than 4 years. He has also been working on various hardware platforms based on the ARM, PPC, and x86 architecture. The diverse nature of subsequent BSPs has challenges in the context of QA. One of the challenges was to keep the QA packages in one place in such a way that they could be applied to all different product/platform combinations. He addressed this by creating a Yocto Project-based layer for which he is a maintainer as well as a gatekeeper.

Acknowledgments

Nothing in this world can be materialized without collective effort. I cannot thank each and everyone behind this success enough.

When this proposal was projected to me, I was unsure whether I could do it. Initially, my dear friend and ex-colleague Shahid Riaz encouraged me to take up this task. I was still not firm about my decision of writing this book, when my mentor, Hazrat-e-Aqdas Shah Abdul Khaliq Azad Raipuri, motivated me to proceed with it. His words have been a source of inspiration for me at every step. I became more confident and completed this book with his prayers and by the grace of Allah.

I would like to thank Shahid Riaz along with his ex-colleague Guila Fourie for reviewing my proposed outline.

I would like to thank my colleagues at Mentor Graphics, Pakistan — Usama Masood, Abbas Raza, Ehson Hussain, and Adeel Arshad — for providing help and support.

I would also like to thank people from Packt with whom I worked. Sonali Vernekar (acquisition editor) was my first point of contact; she is the one who chose me for this work. I had pleasure of working with Mamata Walkar (content development editor), Sageer Parkar and Shipra Chauhan (project coordinators), and Edwin Moses (technical editor). Mamata Walkar was the person I remained in touch with all the time. Thanks for being so cooperative and helpful.

I would like to thank my family members: my extremely caring wife, my son, and my daughter, of course, although I had to wait for her to sleep to do the chores.

About the Reviewers

Daniel Garbanzo Hidalgo is an electronics engineering student from TEC (Tecnológico de Costa Rica). He is 21 years old, speaks Spanish and English, and lives in Cartago, Costa Rica. Electronics, robotics, and technology are his passion, which is the reason he's studying electronics engineering. He is a cofounder/developer of EMSYS Innovations, an electronics systems solutions company. His background and experience cover embedded systems development, digital systems design, verilog hardware description language, several programming languages (C, C++, C#, Python, and assembler), and knowledge of Yocto Project / Linux.

The most important projects that he worked on were basic 2D-3D GPUs developed by the hardware description language on an FPGA, and he also worked on building a classic SNES console with a BeagleBone Black running a customized operating system developed with Yocto Project / Linux. Additionally, he worked on many Arduino and BeagleBone minor projects.

I wish to thank my parents for giving me the opportunity to study for the career of my dreams in the best engineering university of my country and for always being there for me and giving me support.

Noor Ahsan Khawaja works with Mentor Graphics as an engineering manager. He's been working in the software industry for 12 years. He started as a compiler engineer in Mentor Graphics, where he worked on code generation, assemblers, and linkers. In 2009, he started working with OpenEmbedded for Mentor Embedded Linux distributions. Later, OpenEmbedded turned into Yocto Project, and he has been contributing to Yocto Project and the OpenEmbedded community since then. He is maintaining Mentor Graphics' open source layer called meta-mentor. In this layer, he maintains the changes that Mentor would like to have in its Linux distribution. He is working on Yocto Project-based Linux distributions for ARM-, Power-, and x86-based boards.

I would like to thank Irfan Sadiq, the writer of this book, for introducing me as a reviewer. He provided me with an opportunity to review his content to complete this book and take the book to another level of maturity.

Elango Palanisamy, has a bachelor's degree in electronics and communication engineering from Anna University, Chennai. He is currently pursuing master's in embedded system technologies from the same university.

He has experience in firmware, board bring-ups, power management in consumer electronic devices, driver development, and optimizations for thermal printers and car-multimedia-related sensors. He also has experience in using build tools, such as Yocto Project and buildroot for Ti, Freesacle, and Atmel boards.

He is currently working as a platform support engineer in Fossilshale Embedded Technologies Pvt Ltd.

I would like to thank my parents, especially my father, who stood by me through all my hurdles before I was able to attain this position. I would like to thank Mr. Siddiq Ahmed and Mr.Vignesh Rajendran, who have given me this wonderful opportunity of getting into this field. I would also like to thank my friend Ms. Sathya Priya Kumar, who has helped me in reviewing this book.

Ankur Rameshchandra Tank is based in Bangalore, India, and is currently employed with L&T Technology Services. His interests are in the areas of C/C++; Embedded Linux kernel and user space programming; Yocto Project, Bash, and Python scripting; and design patterns.

He has a bachelor's degree in instrumentation and control engineering. His interest in low level drivers and system internals began in college while he was working on a project called *Non-contact type metal sheet thickness measurement using 8051*. He is currently pursuing his master's in embedded system design, wherein he became interested in the Linux device driver and BeagleBone© board development. His master's degree project revolves around his area of interest in the Linux device driver and BeagleBone© board development.

> I had a good time while reviewing this wonderful book, and I would like to take this opportunity to thank my family and friends for all the support they have extended to me.

Mikhail Zakharov works as a radio firmware developer at Cognitive Systems Corporation. In the past, he has worked as an embedded firmware developer at Blackberry, Qualcomm, and ON Semiconductor. He holds a bachelor of applied sciences degree in computer engineering from the University of Waterloo, Canada. His focus is on cellular technologies, hard real-time embedded systems, and FPGA/ASIC development.

www.PacktPub.com

Support files, eBooks, discount offers, and more

For support files and downloads related to your book, please visit
www.PacktPub.com.

Did you know that Packt offers eBook versions of every book published, with PDF
and ePub files available? You can upgrade to the eBook version at www.PacktPub.
com and as a print book customer, you are entitled to a discount on the eBook copy.
Get in touch with us at service@packtpub.com for more details.

At www.PacktPub.com, you can also read a collection of free technical articles,
sign up for a range of free newsletters and receive exclusive discounts and offers on
Packt books and eBooks.

https://www2.packtpub.com/books/subscription/packtlib

Do you need instant solutions to your IT questions? PacktLib is Packt's online digital
book library. Here, you can search, access, and read Packt's entire library of books.

Why subscribe?

- Fully searchable across every book published by Packt
- Copy and paste, print, and bookmark content
- On demand and accessible via a web browser

Free access for Packt account holders

If you have an account with Packt at www.PacktPub.com, you can use this to access
PacktLib today and view 9 entirely free books. Simply use your login credentials for
immediate access.

I dedicate this book to Hazrat-e-Aqdas Shah Saeed Ahmad Raipuri (RA). He is the sole reason for anything positive in me and the rest belongs to me.

Table of Contents

Preface   **vii**

Chapter 1: Welcome to Yocto Project and BeagleBone Black   **1**

Setting up a host environment   **1**

Essentials   2

Graphics   2

Documentation   2

ADT ieinstaller extras   3

Obtaining Yocto Project   **3**

Let's build for BeagleBone   **3**

Local.conf   4

bblayers.conf   6

site.conf   6

auto.conf   6

Trigger build   7

Creating partitions and formatting the SD card   **8**

Copying images to the card   **10**

Hardware setup   **11**

Serial setup   **12**

Booting BeagleBone   **14**

More about configuration files   **15**

machine.conf   15

bitbake.conf   17

Standard target filesystem paths   17

Architecture-dependent build variables   17

Package default variables   17

General work and output directories for the build system   18

Specific image creation and rootfs population information   18

Build flags and options   18

Download locations and utilities	18
Including the rest of the config files	18
Summary	**19**
Chapter 2: What's BitBake All About?	**21**
A brief history of BitBake	**21**
Legacy tools and BitBake	**22**
Cross-compilation	22
Resolving inter-package dependencies	22
Variety of target distribution	22
Coupling to build systems	23
Variety of build systems distros	23
Variety of architecture	23
Exploit parallelism	23
Easy to use, extend, and collaborate	23
BitBake execution	**24**
Parsing metadata	24
Preparing tasklist	25
Executing tasks	25
BitBake options	**26**
Building a specific recipe (-b)	26
Continuing build even in the case of errors (-k, --continue)	27
Force-specific tasks (-f, --force)	27
Using alternate providers (-a, --tryaltconfigs)	27
Executing a specific task (-c)	28
Invalidate stamps (-C, --clear-stamp)	28
Increasing verbosity (-v, --verbose)	28
Debug level (-D, --debug)	29
Dry run (-n, --dry-run)	29
Parse only (-p, --parse-only)	29
Show versions (-s, --show-versions)	29
Get environment (-e, --environment)	29
Generating a dependency graph (-g, --graphviz)	30
Log levels (-l DEBUG_DOMAINS, --log-domains=DEBUG_DOMAINS)	31
Profile (-P, --profile)	31
Select UI (-u UI, --ui=UI)	31
Don't use shared state (--no-setscene)	31
Summary	**32**

Chapter 3: Creating the helloworld Recipe   33

Creating helloworld   33
Contents of the helloworld recipe   36
  Recipe naming and related variables   37
Building a recipe   37
Build directories   39
Tasks   40
  Build   40
  Fetch   40
  Unpack   41
  Patch   41
  Configure   41
  Compile   41
  Install   42
  Package   42
  Devshell   42
  Clean   42
  Cleansstate   42
  Cleanall   43
  Overriding default tasks   43
Deploying helloworld   43
  Manually installing a package   43
  Making an image dependent on our package   44
Summary   44

Chapter 4: Adding Multimedia to Your Board   45

Introducing gaku   45
The recipe for gaku   46
  Package control variables   46
    Build dependencies (DEPENDS)   46
    Runtime dependencies (RDEPENDS)   47
    Runtime recommendations (RRECOMMENDS) 47
    RCONFLICTS   48
    RREPLACE   48
    PROVIDES   48
    RPROVIDES   49
  Source control in a recipe   49
    SRCREV   49
    PV calculation   49
    The SRC_URI specification   50
    The S directory   51
    Inheriting classes   51

GStreamer recipes' short trip   **51**
Types of variable assignments   52
EXTRA_OECONF   53
The FILES_ variables   53
Variable flags   53
ALLOW_EMPTY   53
FILESPATH   54
Conditional overriding mechanisms   54
Reusing and sharing the same code   55
Action time   **55**
Summary   **56**

Chapter 5: Creating and Exploring Layers   **57**
Layer creation using script   **57**
Contents of layers   **60**
The conf directory   60
recipes-* director{y,ies}   63
Classes   64
COPYING.mit   64
README   64
Conditional selection based on layers   **64**
Append files   **65**
Packagegroups   **66**
Summary   **67**

Chapter 6: Your First Console Game   **69**
Hardware requirements   **69**
Pacman4Console   **69**
Let's develop our recipe   **70**
Basic elements   70
Source control   71
Work directory and version   72
The S directory   72
Debugging compile tasks   73
Installing a task   75
Adding package contents   76
Adding a package to the root filesystem   **77**
packagegroup   77
Image bbappend   78
Action   78
Summary   **78**

Chapter 7: Turning BeagleBone into a Home Surveillance System   79
Problem statement   **79**
Requirements   **80**
Existing solutions / literature survey   **80**
  Requiring specialized capturing hardware   80
  Requiring specialized software application   80
  Based on Debian/Angstrom   81
Selected solution   **81**
  Host/server side (BeagleBone)   81
  Client side   82
Let's start the fun   **82**
  Base plugins   82
  Good plugins   83
  Bad plugins   83
  Ugly plugins   83
  Enabling GStreamer and plugins   83
  Enabling Video4Linux2   84
    In-place amendment   85
    Using append   85
    Using local.conf   85
  The GStreamer pipeline   86
Client side   **88**
  VLC   88
  GStreamer   88
Get ready for running and surprises   **88**
  Camera-detection issues   89
  UVC driver DMA issue   90
  Build with the meta-ti layer   90
    Fetch the layer   91
    Set the layer priority   91
    Enable the layer   91
Further enhancements   **92**
Summary   **92**
Chapter 8: BeagleBone as a Wi-Fi Access Point   93
Problem statement / use case   **93**
Requirements   **94**
Literature survey   **94**
Our strategy   **94**

Enabling kernel support   **95**
   Networking support – wireless   95
   Device Drivers > Network device support > Wireless LAN >
   Atheros Wireless Cards   96
   A better approach toward Kernel configurations   96
   Copying firmware   97
   Using the previous kernel version   98
   Issue with rfkill   99
Required packages   **99**
Changing upstart scripts   **100**
Recipe Hotspot-yb   **101**
   The access point launcher script   101
   Systemd service unit file   102
   Configuration file for the driver module   102
   Configuration file for hostapd   102
   The gateway setup file   103
   The udhcp configuration file   103
   The udhcp empty lease file   103
   Recipe file hotspot-yb_0.1.bb   103
Enabling hotspot-yb   **104**
Managing in packagegroups   **105**
Knowing the issues/enhancements   **106**
Summary   **106**
Index   **107**

Preface

Using Yocto Project with BeagleBone Black is intended to be training material for newbies using Yocto Project. For this purpose, the hardware used is BeagleBone.

The book is written keeping reader engagement a top priority. By the end of the first chapter, you will have a working Yocto Project build running on BeagleBone and ready for further experimentation on the host side. Initially, we used existing examples and projects created by Yocto Project scripts to avoid any duplication, save time, and get things functional quickly while performing rigorous changes to learn about multiple scenarios. We won't use graphical tools, even if they are available, in order to avoid making things misleading as well as to avoid a shallow understanding. Also, sometimes, they sometime create confusion by overriding user customizations.

By the end of the book, you will have the necessary skill set, exposure, and experience required to grab any professional grade project based on Yocto Project and BeagleBone.

What this book covers

Chapter 1, Welcome to Yocto Project and BeagleBone Black, enables the user to boot up BeagleBone with images built using Yocto Project through the use of simple instructions.

Chapter 2, What's BitBake All About?, provides a basic introduction to the BitBake tool.

Chapter 3, Creating the helloworld Recipe, talks about a helloworld recipe available in poky. In this chapter, we will use this recipe for the introduction of the basic elements of a recipe.

Chapter 4, Adding Multimedia to Your Board, explores the most common elements encountered in Yocto Project recipes. We will describe each of these elements and their usage.

Chapter 5, Creating and Exploring Layers, teaches you how to override functionalities of recipe files available in the existing layers. We will also look at various techniques used in different scenarios, along with the pros and cons of such techniques.

Chapter 6, Your First Console Game, helps with creating recipes for some of the popular console-based games—for example, MyMan.

Chapter 7, Turning BeagleBone into a Home Surveillance System, teaches you how to create an advanced project using BeagleBone and Yocto Project. We will create a home surveillance solution using a webcam attached to the BeagleBone USB port.

Chapter 8, BeagleBone as a Wi-Fi Access Point, guides you to create an advanced Project using BeagleBone and Yocto Project. We will turn our BeagleBone into a Wi-Fi access point by attaching a USB dongle.

What you need for this book

We will use Python in the book. Any reasonably powerful computer running Ubuntu 12.04 or 14.04 will be suitable. You will need to download and install the following software in your computer:

- Python version 2.7 or higher, excluding Python 3.x

Who this book is for

This book is ideal for system developers with the knowledge and working experience of embedded systems. Knowledge of BeagleBone Black and similar embedded boards is assumed, while no knowledge of the Yocto Project build system is necessary.

Conventions

In this book, you will find a number of text styles that distinguish between different kinds of information. Here are some examples of these styles and an explanation of their meaning.

Code words in text, database table names, folder names, filenames, file extensions, pathnames, dummy URLs, user input, and Twitter handles are shown as follows: "We have seen the SRC_URI variable in our recipe."

A block of code is set as follows:

```
do_<taskname>() {
   :
}
```

Any command-line input or output is written as follows:

```
# cp /usr/src/asterisk-addons/configs/cdr_mysql.conf.sample
    /etc/asterisk/cdr_mysql.conf
```

New terms and **important words** are shown in bold. Words that you see on the screen, for example, in menus or dialog boxes, appear in the text like this: "Choose **Save setup as dfl** to avoid reconfiguring every time and choose **Exit** to go to minicom."

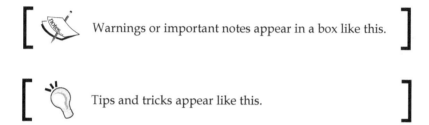

Warnings or important notes appear in a box like this.

Tips and tricks appear like this.

Reader feedback

Feedback from our readers is always welcome. Let us know what you think about this book—what you liked or disliked. Reader feedback is important for us as it helps us develop titles that you will really get the most out of.

To send us general feedback, simply e-mail feedback@packtpub.com, and mention the book's title in the subject of your message.

If there is a topic that you have expertise in and you are interested in either writing or contributing to a book, see our author guide at www.packtpub.com/authors.

Customer support

Now that you are the proud owner of a Packt book, we have a number of things to help you to get the most from your purchase.

Downloading the example code

Most of the implementation code is kept at `https://github.com/YoctoForBeaglebone/` and can be pulled directly from there. If you have something to add, feel free to add it. While adding something to any repository, kindly avoid pushing directly to the repository and use Git pull request mechanism supported by GitHub.

Downloading the color images of this book

We also provide you with a PDF file that has color images of the screenshots/diagrams used in this book. The color images will help you better understand the changes in the output. You can download this file from `http://www.packtpub.com/sites/default/files/downloads/1234OT_ColorImages.pdf`.

Errata

Although we have taken every care to ensure the accuracy of our content, mistakes do happen. If you find a mistake in one of our books—maybe a mistake in the text or the code—we would be grateful if you could report this to us. By doing so, you can save other readers from frustration and help us improve subsequent versions of this book. If you find any errata, please report them by visiting `http://www.packtpub.com/submit-errata`, selecting your book, clicking on the **Errata Submission Form** link, and entering the details of your errata. Once your errata are verified, your submission will be accepted and the errata will be uploaded to our website or added to any list of existing errata under the Errata section of that title.

To view the previously submitted errata, go to `https://www.packtpub.com/books/content/support` and enter the name of the book in the search field. The required information will appear under the **Errata** section.

Piracy

Piracy of copyrighted material on the Internet is an ongoing problem across all media. At Packt, we take the protection of our copyright and licenses very seriously. If you come across any illegal copies of our works in any form on the Internet, please provide us with the location address or website name immediately so that we can pursue a remedy.

Please contact us at `copyright@packtpub.com` with a link to the suspected pirated material.

We appreciate your help in protecting our authors and our ability to bring you valuable content.

Questions

If you have a problem with any aspect of this book, you can contact us at `questions@packtpub.com`, and we will do our best to address the problem.

1
Welcome to Yocto Project and BeagleBone Black

In this chapter, we will discuss how we can use Yocto Project to bring up BeagleBone. We will discuss the steps that are necessary to set up a host environment for Yocto Project, create images, and set up BeagleBone hardware. We will also discuss how to prepare a card and finally deploy images on the board. Fortunately, BeagleBone is one of the reference boards of Yocto Project, and it makes our lives easier. We can find the core steps for hardware setup in `README.hardware`, under Poky. There is a lot of information in the Yocto Project Development Reference Manual. What will we be doing here then? The steps given under Poky assume a lot of previous knowledge and sometimes a great deal of generic approach is used there, which isn't very useful for us. We will simplify things here. During this journey, we will pay a visit to different configuration files of Yocto Project and try to develop an understanding of these files. In this chapter, we will:

- Set up a host environment
- Obtain Yocto Project
- Build for BeagleBone
- Learn about configuration files

Setting up a host environment

Before we start getting sources for Yocto Project and building it, we need to prepare our host system. Yocto Project is supposed to work on any distribution of Linux known to us. There is a list of supported platforms available in the *Yocto Project Reference Manual* (`http://www.yoctoproject.org/docs/current/ref-manual/ref-manual.html#intro-requirements`).

That is not to say that Yocto Project will not work on other distributions, but the given distributions are the ones on which it is verified to work successfully.

- Ubuntu 12.04 (LTS)
- Ubuntu 13.10
- Ubuntu 14.04 (LTS)
- Fedora release 19 (Schrödinger's Cat)
- Fedora release 20 (Heisenbug)
- CentOS release 6.4, 6.5
- Debian GNU/Linux 7.0, 7.1, 7.2, 7.3, and 7.4 (Wheezy)
- openSUSE 12.2, 12.3, and 13.1

For Poky Daisy 1.6.1, the list is long. We will stick to Ubuntu 14.04 (LTS) for the rest of the book. For this release, package dependencies that need to be taken care of are divided into the following four subcategories.

Essentials

These are the core tools and packages that are required to build Yocto Project. These include a GNU compiler, versioning control system, and other packages that are required to build an environment on host. Here's the command to get the essentials:

```
$ sudo apt-get install gawk wget git-core diffstat unzip texinfo gcc-multilib \
    build-essential chrpath
```

Graphics

If you want to use graphics support or you intend to use Eclipse IDE, then you need to install these packages:

```
$ sudo apt-get install libsdl1.2-dev xterm
```

Documentation

These packages are required if you want to build a Yocto Project documentation:

```
$ sudo apt-get install make xsltproc docbook-utils fop dblatex xmlto
```

ADT Installer Extras

These packages are required only if you want to build an Application Development Kit (ADK):

```
$ sudo apt-get install autoconf automake libtool libglib2.0-dev
```

If you are using any distribution other than those previously listed, you will find similar commands can be used on Debian distributions, as well. For other supported distributions, consult the *Yocto Project Reference Manual*.

Obtaining Yocto Project

We will use the daisy branch of Poky, which is a name for 1.6.1 version of Yocto Project. We will stick to this version throughout this book. These are the steps to follow while obtaining Yocto Project:

1. First, create a folder called `yocto`. Then, create a directory for it:

   ```
   $ mkdir yocto
   ```

2. Change the directory to this newly created directory:

   ```
   $ cd yocto
   ```

3. Fetch sources for Poky:

   ```
   $ git clone -b daisy git://git.yoctoproject.org/poky.git
   ```

4. Change the directory to `poky`:

   ```
   $ cd poky
   ```

What is the next logical step? Have a look at the directory contents using the `ls` command to see what we got. Welcome! We are in good place. Let's enjoy our journey.

Let's build for BeagleBone

By examining the contents of the `poky` directory, you will notice your terminal executables, as in most of the cases while working with new technologies/packages on *nix systems. Here, we have `oe-init-build-env`. This is the one responsible for creating our build environment. We will source this script and pass to it our build directory as an argument, as follows:

```
$ source oe-init-build-env build_bbb
```

The `build_bbb` argument can be anything you want. I wanted to keep it simply bbb. However, I cannot do this as my Git Aware Prompt keeps complaining about new content. If you inspect `.gitignore`, you will see that it has `build*` in it. So, the directory prefixed with build will be ignored. This command will land you in the newly created build directory. Before moving further, we need to examine this directory. Here, we have a subdirectory named `conf` and two files, `bblayers.conf` and `local.conf`. We will look into `bblayers.conf` in the upcoming chapters. For now, we will go through the contents of `local.conf`.

Local.conf

First, we will encounter the following two options, which are related to each other. These options are here to tune the level of parallelism used by BitBake, the actual driver behind Yocto Project. The two options are:

- `BB_NUMBER_THREADS ?= "${@oe.utils.cpu_count()}"`
- `PARALLEL_MAKE ?= "-j ${@oe.utils.cpu_count()}"`

You will find these variables twice in this file: once in the preceding form and once in the following form:

```
#BB_NUMBER_THREADS ?= "4"
#PARALLEL_MAKE ?= "-j 4"
```

We are telling BitBake about the maximum number of threads it should use for the job and the maximum of jobs run in parallel. Most of the Yocto Project manuals and blogs say both of these should be equal to the number of cores available on your system. However, my experience has proven that the following formula gives the maximum throughput, that is, the minimum time of execution:

```
BB_NUMBER_THREADS ?= "1.5 * Number of cores"
PARALLEL_MAKE ?= "-j 2 * Number of cores"
```

On a 16-core server, we will use the combinations of 24 and 32, whereas on an 8-core machine we will use 12 and 16. For a 4-core machine, we will use 6 and 8 as follows:

```
BB_NUMBER_THREADS ?= "6"
PARALLEL_MAKE ?= "-j 8"
```

 While setting these variables, do not forget the difference of `-j n` for `PARALLE_MAKE`. Otherwise, you will encounter errors. Also, note that BitBake requires even numbers to be enclosed in `""`.

Next, we need to select the machine. Here, we will set BeagleBone, which is already available to us. So, we will uncomment it and comment out the default selection, which is the qemux86 selection. Commenting out an existing selection is not strictly necessary since it is assigned using the `??` operator, which we will discuss in the upcoming chapters.

```
MACHINE ?= "beaglebone"
#MACHINE ??= "qemux86"
```

Next, we will set our `downloads` directory. This directory will be used to download sources for packages. The available configuration variable to set this configuration is `DL_DIR`. If we don't set this, its default value would be used as our build directory. So, we will have this directory created under the build directory. We usually don't care much in case of **Board Support Packages** (**BSPs**) running `rm-rf` on our build directory to start a fresh build. In such cases, not caring about this variable can cause regrets, as it will download all the sources again and again, causing longer build times. We set it up in the top-level directory, which contains the `poky` directory itself, so that we don't ever accidentally delete it with other expendable stuff.

```
DL_DIR ?= "${TOPDIR}/../../downloads"
```

Next, we have `SSTATE_DIR`, `TMPDIR`, and `DISTRO`, which we will leave unchanged for now. `SSTATE_DIR` is related to the shared state feature of Yocto Project. Yocto Project has a mechanism to check whether some package is already built and available, it uses the existing package and doesn't build it. `TMPDIR` is the directory that contains a lot of build stuff. We will go through its contents in the upcoming chapters. Then, we have `PACKAGE_CLASSES`, as follow:

```
PACKAGE_CLASSES ?= "package_ipk"
```

We will leave the remaining variables unchanged.

We can use a lot other options in this file as well. We will learn about some of these options in the upcoming chapters.

While setting values for a variable, always remember to leave spaces on both sides of an operator in order to avoid any surprises.

bblayers.conf

As the name suggests, `bblayers.conf` is there to provide us with a mechanism to configure our Yocto Project layers. This file has configurations related to layers. We can add extra layers to this file to use the metadata available in these layers. This file further classifies layers into removable and non-removable ones, as you can see in the following code snippet:

```
BBLAYERSBBLAYERSBBLAYERS ?= " \
  /home/irfan/yocto/poky/meta \
  /home/irfan/yocto/poky/meta-yocto \
  /home/irfan/yocto/poky/meta-yocto-bsp \
  "
BBLAYERS_NON_REMOVABLE ?= " \
  /home/irfan/yocto/poky/meta \
  /home/irfan/yocto/poky/meta-yocto \
  "
```

Since we are not using any extra layers, we will leave this file unchanged.

site.conf

This file is optional. You won't find it created by the build environment creation script. We mostly use system-wide or other configurations common across different builds and targets are put in this file. For example, we would use the toolchain path if we were using an external toolchain. Another option could be specifying mirror sites, we case it for this purpose. If we have this file created, BitBake looks for it and uses common configurations from this file. We override any configuration that we want modified in `conf/local.conf`.

auto.conf

This is an optional file. Just like the previous file, you won't find it created by the build environment creation script. We can use this file to set our custom options so that we don't have to modify `local.conf` manually. In most of the cases, this file is used by build systems such as Jenkins. For example, if we don't want our build directory size to explode due to space constraints, we could use the following code file in the `local.conf` or `auto.conf` file:

```
INHERIT += "rm_work"
```

For now, we don't need to set this. I am just mentioning it here to elaborate the preceding point. Since we will analyze the contents of the `tmp/work` directory in the upcoming chapters, I would suggest that you do not use this option for the time being.

Trigger build

Now that we have set all the configurations, let's start our build. You can choose any of the images to build. I will prefer `core-image-sato`:

```
$  bitbake core-image-sato
```

Building images for our desired target may take some time, depending on network speed and processing power. After the build is complete, you will have your images ready at `tmp/deploy/images/beaglebone/` under your build directory, as shown in the following screenshot. This contains first-level bootloader MLO, second-level bootloader u-boot, kernel image, device tree blobs, a root filesystem archive, and a modules archive.

Here, you will notice that we have symbolic links as well as full names of the files, with time stamp information in most of the cases. Symbolic links always point to the latest file created. We should always try to use a symbolic link for copying to avoid any confusion.

Now that we have our images created by Yocto Project, we are ready to verify these images on our BeagleBone board:

Images directory contents

In case of other images, such as core-image-minimal, core-image-base, and core-image-sdk, the content shown in this screenshot will contain files related to those images instead of `core-image-sato`.

Creating partitions and formatting the SD card

BeagleBone Black is shipped with Angstrom images by default and partitioned as we require. However, if you have damaged it or don't want to erase the default images, then you should follow these instructions to prepare another BeagleBone for use.

If the card you have inserted has some partitions, they will be mounted automatically. To avoid any surprises like damaging the card, unmount these partitions. If you are using an SD card reader, the device for the card will be /dev/mmcblk*. If you are using some USB card reader, then the device will be something like /dev/sdX, where X is a number. X depends on the SCSI drives that are already connected to your system. We are using the first option, that is, a built-in SD card reader. You can determine which device is created for your card by issuing the dmesg command as follows:

```
$ dmesg | tail
[27409.486378] mmc0: new high speed SDHC card at address 0007
[27409.486640] mmcblk0: mmc0:0007 SD04G 3.70 GiB
[27409.488506]  mmcblk0: p1
```

You can also use fdisk -1 to check what device is created for your card. Now, you can use the fdisk utility as root or with sudo to create our required partitions, using the following steps:

1. Unmount any mounted partition, using the umount command:

   ```
   $ umount /dev/mmcblk0p1
   ```

2. Launch the fdisk utitility and delete the previous partition(s); in our case, it is just one:

   ```
   $ sudo fdisk /dev/mmcblk0
   Command (m for help): d
   Selected partition 1
   ```

3. Create new partition called BOOT of 32 MB and type primary:

   ```
   Command (m for help): n
   Partition type:
      p   primary (0 primary, 0 extended, 4 free)
      e   extended
   Select (default p):
   Using default response p
   ```

```
Partition number (1-4, default 1):
Using default value 1
First sector (2048-7774207, default 2048):
Using default value 2048
Last sector, +sectors or +size{K,M,G} (2048-7774207, default
7774207): +32M
```

4. Create a second partition to hold `rootfs`. We will give all the remaining space to this partition:

```
Command (m for help): n
Partition type:
    p   primary (1 primary, 0 extended, 3 free)
    e   extended
Select (default p):
Using default response p
Partition number (1-4, default 2):
Using default value 2
First sector (67584-7774207, default 67584):
Using default value 67584
Last sector, +sectors or +size{K,M,G} (67584-7774207, default
7774207):
Using default value 7774207
```

5. Make the first partition bootable by setting the boot flag:

```
Command (m for help): a
Partition number (1-4): 1
```

6. Set the first partition as WIN95 FAT32 (LBA):

```
Command (m for help): t
Selected partition 1
Hex code (type L to list codes): c
```

7. We are done with the filesystem modification. So, let's write it by issuing the w command:

```
Command (m for help): w
The partition table has been altered!
Calling ioctl() to re-read partition table.
Syncing disks.
```

> Do not forget to set the first partition as WIN95 FAT32 (LBA); otherwise, BeagleBone won't be able to boot from it. In this case, you might end up wasting time figuring out what's going wrong.

8. Format the first partition as FAT, using the following command. We will set the label as BOOT so that we know what directory it will be mounted to by udisks:

```
$ sudo mkfs.vfat -n "BOOT" /dev/mmcblk0p1
```

9. Format the second partition as an ext4 filesystem, using the following command. The label for this is set to ROOT, as it will contain the extracted image of rootfs.

```
$ sudo mkfs.ext4 -L "ROOT" /dev/mmcblk0p2
```

I have created a simple script to perform all the preceding steps. I am listing these steps here for your understanding, so that you can do any adjustments if required.

> **Downloading the example code**
>
> Most of the implementation code is kept at https://github.com/YoctoForBeaglebone/ and can be pulled directly from there. If you have something to add, feel free to add it. While adding something to any repository, kindly avoid pushing directly to the repository and use Git pull request mechanism supported by GitHub.

Copying images to the card

We have formatted our card, according to the requirements. Now, we are ready to populate images to it. The partitions are usually auto mounted under /media/$USER. If not, we can use the mount command to mount the partition to our desired location:

```
$ sudo mount /dev/sdb1 /media/$USER/BOOT
$ sudo mount /dev/sdb2 /media/$USER/ROOT
```

Now, follow these steps to copy images to the card:

1. Copy the u-boot MLO and u-boot bootloader images into the FAT32 partition:

   ```
   $ sudo cp MLO /media/$USER/BOOT
   ```

   ```
   $ sudo cp u-boot.img /media/$USER/BOOT
   ```

2. Copy the kernel image into the boot partition:

   ```
   $ sudo cp uImage /media/$USER/BOOT
   ```

3. Copy the `.dtb` file, `am335x-boneblack.dtb`, into the boot partition. This step is required only in the case of `core-image-minimal`. It is not required in our case, as we created `core-image-sato`, which already has this file placed at the desired location in rootfs:

   ```
   $ sudo cp am335x-boneblack.dtb /media/$USER/BOOT
   ```

4. As a root user, uncompress `core-image-sato-beaglebone.tar.bz2` to the `ext4` partition:

   ```
   $ sudo tar -xf core-image-sato-beaglebone.tar.bz2 -C
   /media/$USER/ROOT/
   ```

5. Unmount both partitions:

   ```
   $ sudo umount /dev/mmcblk0p1
   ```

   ```
   $ sudo umount /dev/mmcblk0p2
   ```

Remove the card from the host machine, and insert it into the SD card slot on BeagleBone Black. We have a simple script named `copy_images.sh` for these steps as well.

> You can download the script for copying images the SD card from here:
> `https://github.com/YoctoForBeaglebone/BeagleScripts`

Hardware setup

To boot BeagleBone Black, we need the following hardware:

- An SD card with images flashed
- BeagleBone Black

- A power adapter that can supply 5V or a micro USB cable; we should use a 5V power adapter in order to avoid a decrease in the operating frequency
- USB TTL-2303(PL2303) for serial communication

USB-TTL is connected to the J1 connector of BeagleBone in the following formation:

J1 Pin	USB TTL Function
1	GND Ground
4	RXL
5	TXL

A micro USB cable should be enough in most of the cases to provide power. However, for more resource-intensive tasks, for example, if additional peripherals are required, you will need to connect a power adapter.

 Be careful when using PL2303 pins for current; otherwise, you may end up damaging your BeagleBone.

Serial setup

BeagleBone Black uses a serial debug port to communicate with the host machine. We will use minicom as a serial terminal client to communicate over the serial port. To set up minicom, perform the following steps:

1. Run this setup command as a privileged user:

```
$  sudo minicom -s
```

Mmicom main configuration dialogue

A menu will appear on the terminal with nine different options, as shown in the preceding screenshot. We won't be changing many of these. The up and down arrow keys can be used to select these options. We will select the third option, **Serial port setup**. Choose this option by pressing the *Enter* key. You will enter into another menu in which each option is listed, along with a corresponding key on the keyboard on the left-hand side to choose the option. Press the *A* key on the keyboard to set your serial device to /dev/ ttyUSB0, and then press *Enter*. If you are not sure which device is created in your case, you could find this out by using the following command combination on another terminal:

```
$ dmesg | grep "pl2303 converter"
[37532.385583] pl2303 3-3:1.0: pl2303 converter detected
[37532.386415] usb 3-3: pl2303 converter now attached to ttyUSB0
```

2. Press *E* to set the baud rate. Use the *A* and *B* keys to navigate the baud rate values. *A* corresponds to next and *B* to previous. Keep pressing *B* till you get 115200 8N1. Then, press *Enter* to choose this setting and go back to the previous menu.

3. Next, we need to press *F* and *G* to change enablement statuses of hardware flow control and software flow control. Both need to be set to **No**. Finally, the settings should look as shown in this screenshot:

```
+-------------------------------------------------------------------+
| A -     Serial Device      : /dev/ttyUSB0                         |
| B - Lockfile Location      : /var/lock                            |
| C -     Callin Program     :                                      |
| D -   Callout Program      :                                      |
| E -      Bps/Par/Bits      : 115200 8N1                           |
| F - Hardware Flow Control  : No                                   |
| G - Software Flow Control  : No                                   |
|                                                                   |
|   Change which setting? ▊                                         |
+-------------------------------------------------------------------+
        | Screen and keyboard    |
        | Save setup as dfl      |
        | Save setup as..        |
        | Exit                   |
        | Exit from Minicom      |
        +------------------------+
```

Minicom Serial Port Setup dialogue

4. Choose **Save setup as dfl** to avoid reconfiguring every time and choose **Exit** to go to minicom. Don't exit from it if you want to observe whether there is any activity on the serial port.

Booting BeagleBone

Now that we have everything set up, we are ready to boot. We can just insert this card, and our board should boot from it. There might be only one issue if you have the **eMMC (embedded MultiMediaCard)** boot selected by default. You will have to disable it by booting up the board from the images you already have and renaming the MLO file from the eMMC partition. Alternatively, you can simply execute the following two commands on the u-boot prompt. To stop at the u-boot prompt, simply press *Enter* after powering up the board before timeout:

```
# mmc dev 1
# mmc erase 0 512
```

The first command will select the eMMC card, and the second one will do the erasing so that BeagleBone doesn't try to boot from eMMC.

Insert our prepared SD card and power up BeagleBone. You should get an output similar to the following one on minicom:

```
Booting from mmc ...
## Booting kernel from Legacy Image at 82000000 ...
    Image Name:    Linux-3.14.0-yocto-standard
    Image Type:    ARM Linux Kernel Image (uncompressed)
    Data Size:     4985768 Bytes = 4.8 MiB
    Load Address: 80008000
    Entry Point:   80008000
    Verifying Checksum ... OK
## Flattened Device Tree blob at 88000000
    Booting using the fdt blob at 0x88000000
    Loading Kernel Image ... OK
    Loading Device Tree to 8fff5000, end 8ffff207 ... OK
Starting kernel …
```

Finally, we will land in our BeagleBone prompt:

```
Poky (Yocto Project Reference Distro) 1.6.1 beaglebone /dev/ttyO0
beaglebone login:
```

Enter root as user, and you are in as the root user:

```
root@beaglebone:~#
```

More about configuration files

We have already visited some configuration files during the build process. There are some more configuration files that were not discussed during the build process in order to avoid making it lengthier. These are `bitbake.conf` and `machine.conf`. Let's look at them.

machine.conf

You won't find a file with this name. Here, machine is a placeholder for the target board we are preparing our images for. For example, in our case, this file is `beaglebone.conf` and in the preceding configuration, it is available as `beaglebone.conf` in the `poky/meta-yocto-bsp/conf/machine/` directory.

All of the machine- specific configurations are done in this file. We need to know about it and have some basic understanding of its contents so that we can modify it, if required. Let's go through it. The top-level header contains information in tags for documentation:

```
#@TYPE: Machine
#@NAME: Beaglebone machine
#@DESCRIPTION: Machine configuration for http://beagleboard.org/bone
and http://beagleboard.org/black boards
```

The preferred xserver can be used:

```
PREFERRED_PROVIDER_virtual/xserver ?= "xserver-xorg"
XSERVER ?= "xserver-xorg \
            xf86-input-evdev \
            xf86-input-mouse \
            xf86-video-fbdev \
            xf86-input-keyboard"
```

What extra recipes need to be built? These are built here:

```
MACHINE_EXTRA_RRECOMMENDS = " kernel-modules kernel-devicetree"
```

Set image dependencies:

```
EXTRA_IMAGEDEPENDS += "u-boot"
```

Architecture-specific configurations are found in tune files. Here, we will set the available one that will fulfill our requirements:

```
DEFAULTTUNE ?= "cortexa8hf-neon"
include conf/machine/include/tune-cortexa8.inc
```

These tune files are present under Poky on the path that we are using in `include` directive.

Here, we will specify the type of filesystem images we want to create for our machine. There are other options to choose from. Also, here, we will set extra image commands in the case of the `jffs2` image:

```
IMAGE_FSTYPES += "tar.bz2 jffs2"
EXTRA_IMAGECMD_jffs2 = "-lnp "
```

One of the most important options is the serial debug console. Here, we are defining our eyes with which to peek inside the board:

```
SERIAL_CONSOLE = "115200 ttyO0"
```

Here, we are tweaking our kernel options to see what recipe should be used for kernel compilation and what version of kernel needs to be built. For this, we will use the Yocto Project keywords, `PREFERRED_PROVIDER` and `PREFERRED_VERSION`:

```
PREFERRED_PROVIDER_virtual/kernel ?= "linux-yocto"
PREFERRED_VERSION_linux-yocto ?= "3.14%"
```

We can also create another kernel image, zImage. Since this is a generic machine for BeagleBone Black and White versions, we will create device tree binary files for both of the target. You can opt not to build DTB for BeagleBone White, but this won't make much difference in terms of build time or cleanliness, if you are considering such things. Also, we can set any extra arguments that need to be passed to `KERNEL`:

```
KERNEL_IMAGETYPE = "uImage"
KERNEL_DEVICETREE = "am335x-bone.dtb am335x-boneblack.dtb"
KERNEL_EXTRA_ARGS += "LOADADDR=${UBOOT_ENTRYPOINT}"
```

Here, we will configure most of the aspects of our bootloaders. We will set MLO as the binary name for stage-one bootloader so that we will have it created as MLO, as we saw in the images directory. We will specify a u-boot suffix, `img`, to be used so that we have the `u-boot.img` file created. Other options are also related to u-boot, such as these:

```
SPL_BINARY = "MLO"
UBOOT_SUFFIX = "img"
UBOOT_MACHINE = "am335x_evm_config"
UBOOT_ENTRYPOINT = "0x80008000"
UBOOT_LOADADDRESS = "0x80008000"
```

Now, we will determine the features that we want our machine to support or, more precisely, the features it has the ability to support. We will also determine which features we want turn on:

```
MACHINE_FEATURES = "usbgadget usbhost vfat alsa"
```

bitbake.conf

As the name signifies, this file is related to BitBake, the real engine behind Yocto Project, which is responsible for the simplification of our build process. This file is parsed first and then the rest of the configuration files listed in it are parsed. This file is found under `poky/meta/conf/ as bitbake.conf`. This is not a small file, so we cannot go through it line by line. It contains more than 700 lines of configuration and metadata. Almost all the metadata used in our recipes is defined in this file.

It is not a standalone file. Instead, it includes other files from the `conf` directory. We can find all the files that were described earlier in it. So, `bitbake.conf` uses these files and the metadata definitions in them. For example, if you remember, we used some variables such as `DL_DIR`, `TOPDIR`, and `TMPDIR`, You can find all these variables in this file, along with their default values. This file has all the metadata arranged in different sections. It contains about 20 different sections. Variables defined in one section are used in other sections. Let's have a brief look at some of these sections.

Standard target filesystem paths

These are standard filesystem paths extensively used in different recipes. This section has further subsections. You won't need to change these variables, but you should reference these while developing recipes.

Architecture-dependent build variables

This is also a huge set of variables to define architecture-dependent metadata. These variables are prefixed with `BUILD_`, `HOST_`, `TARGET_`, and `SDK_` so as to clarify their domain of affect.

Package default variables

Variables from this section are extensively used in recipes. These variables are used in every recipe. We will discuss most of these variables in the upcoming chapters.

General work and output directories for the build system

We have touched some of these variables while configuring our build. These define most of the build directory structure. This section contains a staging-related section. This section is very important for cross compilation, which is usually the case when using Yocto Project.

Specific image creation and rootfs population information

These variables define different properties of our root filesystem image. For example, from variables such as IMAGE_NAME, you can infer how the name of our image, core-image-sato-beaglebone-20141126124205, is created.

Build flags and options

Of course, our build flags go into this section. You can see different flags related to compiler, linker, and Make in this section.

Download locations and utilities

This section contains mirror definitions for speeding up the build process. Since we are creating BSPs that contain a lot of packages, we face time constraints. Yocto Project tries to tackle such obstacles in this way. Also, you can see commands to fetch from different versioning systems in this section.

Including the rest of the config files

As we already discussed, this file includes other configuration files. Here, you can see the list of these files.

To avoid wasting time, I am skipping the other sections. You can have a look at them at your leisure.

Summary

In this chapter, you learned how to prepare our host system to use it as a Yocto Project development host. You also learned how to build BeagleBone images using Yocto Project, prepare an SD card, boot the board from this card, and set up serial communication to the board to take a sneak peek into it. We discussed most of the configuration files in this chapter. We took a brief look at some extra configuration files, as well. In the next chapter, you will learn about the core tool behind Yocto Project, which is BitBake, in detail. You will also learn about its various options and how we can use them to make our lives easier.

2
What's BitBake All About?

In the previous chapter, we created a working image for BeagleBone using Yocto Project. We also briefly discussed the different concepts while working on the exercises. In this chapter, we will move one step ahead by detailing different aspects of the basic engine behind Yocto Project, and other similar projects. This engine is BitBake. Covering all the various aspects of BitBake in one chapter is not possible; it will require a complete book. We will familiarize you as much as possible with this tool.

We will cover the following topics in this chapter:

- A brief history of BitBake
- Legacy tools and BitBake
- Execution of BitBake
- BitBake options

A brief history of BitBake

BitBake drew inspiration from the Gentoo package management tool, Portage. Gentoo has a unique philosophy of building binaries on the system where they are supposed to run, so that maximum optimizations can be applied to the code. This philosophy fits best in the case of embedded systems, where you always have a different set of hardware in hand, and you need to prepare board support packages for that hardware. Initially, BitBake was a part of OpenEmbedded.

Later on, an OpenEmbedded project team member, Chris Larson, split it into two separate pieces:

- **BitBake**: This is a generic task executor
- **OpenEmbedded**: This is a metadata set utilized by BitBake

Now, BitBake is the base for OpenEmbedded and Yocto Project, which are being used to build and maintain multiple Linux distributions.

Legacy tools and BitBake

This discussion does not intend to invoke any religious row between other alternatives and BitBake. Every step in the evolution has its own importance, which cannot be denied, and so do other available tools. BitBake was developed keeping in mind the Embedded Linux Development domain. So, it tried to solve the problems faced in this core area, and in my opinion, it addresses these in the best way till date. You might get the same output using other tools, such as Buildroot, but the flexibility and ease provided by BitBake in this domain is second to none. The major difference is in addressing the problem. Legacy tools are developed considering packages in mind, but BitBake evolved to solve the problems faced during the creation of BSPs, or embedded distributions. Let's go through the challenges faced in this specific domain and understand how BitBake helps us face them.

Cross-compilation

BitBake takes care of cross compilation. You do not have to worry about it for each package you are building. You can use the same set of packages and build for different platforms seamlessly.

Resolving inter-package dependencies

This is the real pain of resolving dependencies of packages on each other and fulfilling them. In this case, we need to specify the different dependency types available, and BitBake takes care of them for us. We can handle both build and runtime dependencies.

Variety of target distribution

BitBake supports a variety of target distribution creations. We can define a full new distribution of our own, by choosing package management, image types, and other artifacts to fulfill our requirements.

Coupling to build systems

BitBake is not very dependent on the build system we use to build our target images. We don't use libraries and tools installed on the system; we build their native versions and use them instead. This way, we are not dependent on the build system's root filesystem.

Variety of build systems distros

Since BitBake is very loosely coupled to the build system's distribution type, it's very easy to use on various distributions.

Variety of architecture

We have to support different architectures. We don't have to modify our recipes for each package. We can write our recipes so that features, parameters, and flags are picked up conditionally.

Exploit parallelism

For the simplest projects, we have to build images and do more than a thousand tasks. These tasks require us to use the full power available to us, whether they are computational or related to memory. BitBake's architecture supports us in this regard, using its scheduler to run as many tasks in parallel as it can, or as we configure. Also, when we say task, it should not be confused with package, but it is a part of package. A package can contain many tasks, (fetch, compile, configure, package, `populate_sysroot`, and so on), and all these can run in parallel.

Easy to use, extend, and collaborate

Keeping and relying on metadata keeps things simple and configurable. Almost nothing is hard coded. Thus, we can configure things according to our requirements. Also, BitBake provides us with a mechanism to reuse things that are already developed. We can keep our metadata structured, so that it gets applied/extended conditionally. You will learn these tricks when we will explore layers.

BitBake execution

To get us to a successful package or image, BitBake performs some steps that we need to go through to get an understanding of the workflow. In certain cases, some of these steps can be avoided; but we are not discussing such cases, considering them as corner cases. For details on these, we should refer to the BitBake user manual.

Parsing metadata

When we invoke the BitBake command to build our image, the first thing it does is parse our base configuration metadata. This metadata, as we have already seen in the previous chapter, consists of `build_bb/conf/bblayers.conf`, `multiple layer/conf/layer.conf`, and `poky/meta/conf/bitbake.conf`. This data can be of the following types:

- Configuration data
- Class data
- Recipes

Key variables `BBFILES` and `BBPATH`, which are constructed from the `layer.conf` file. Thus, the constructed `BBPATH` variable is used to locate configuration files under `conf/` and class files under `class/` directories. The `BBFILES` variable is used to find recipe files (`.bb` and `.bbappend`). We have discussed `bblayers.conf` in the previous chapter. It is used to set these variables.

Next, the `bitbake.conf` file is parsed, which also has been discussed in the previous chapter.

 If there is no `bblayers.conf` file, it is assumed that the user has set `BBFILES` and `BBPATH` directly in the environment.

After having dealt with configuration files, class files inclusion and parsing are taken care of. These class files are specified using the `INHERIT` variable. Next, BitBake will use the `BBFILES` variable to construct a list of recipes to parse, along with any append files. Thus, after parsing, recipe values for various variables are stored into datastore. After the completion of a recipe parsing BitBake has:

- A list of tasks that the recipe has defined
- A set of data consisting of keys and values
- Dependency information of the tasks

Preparing tasklist

BitBake starts looking through the PROVIDES set in recipe files. The PROVIDES set defaults to the recipe name, and we can define multiple values to it. We can have multiple recipes providing a similar package. This task is accomplished by setting PROVIDES in the recipes. While actually making such recipes part of the build, we have to define PRREFERED_PROVIDER_foo so that our specific recipe foo can be used. We can do this in multiple locations. In the case of kernels, we use it in the manchin. conf file. BitBake iterates through the list of targets it has to build and resolves them, along with their dependencies.

If PRREFERED_PROVIDER is not set and multiple versions of a package exist, BitBake will choose the highest version.

Each target/recipe has multiple tasks, such as fetch, unpack, configure, and compile. BitBake considers each of these tasks as independent units to exploit parallelism in a multicore environment, which you learned to configure in the previous chapter. Although these tasks are executed sequentially for a single package/recipe, for multiple packages, they are run in parallel. We may be compiling one recipe, configuring the second, and unpacking the third in parallel. Or, may be at the start, eight packages are all fetching their sources. For now, we should know the dependencies between tasks that are defined using DEPENDS and RDEPENDS. In DEPENDS, we provide the dependencies that our package needs to build successfully. So, BitBake takes care of building these dependencies before our package is built. RDEPENDS are the dependencies that are required for our package to execute/run successfully on the target system. So, BitBake takes care of providing these dependencies on the target's root filesystem.

Executing tasks

Tasks can be defined using the shell syntax or Python. In the case of shell tasks, a shell script is created under a temporary directory as run.do_taskname.pid and then, it is executed. The generated shell script contains all the exported variables and the shell functions, with all the variables expanded. Output from the task is saved in the same directory with log.do_taskname.pid. In the case of errors, BitBake shows the full path to this logfile. This is helpful for debugging.

BitBake options

BitBake also follows the standard of the -h or --help option. So, anytime, we can list all the available options by running BitBake with any of these options. Thus, we won't get into their details. We will try to discuss only those options that we will encounter most, or we need the most. Another standard or generic option is to get the --version version of BitBake, which is also available. We used the simplest form of BitBake in the previous chapter to build our images:

```
$ bitbake core-image-sato
```

Here, core-image-sato was the name of the image recipe we were building.

The format of bitbake command as inferred from bitbake -h is as follows:

```
Usage: bitbake [options] [recipe name/target ...]
```

In the preceding example, we did not provide any option, as it was not required in the scenario we were building.

Now, issue BitBake with -h, as shown here from the build directory that we created in the first chapter:

```
$ bitbake -h
```

We will skip the output here due to the length and discuss some important options.

Building a specific recipe (-b)

In some cases, we need to build only one recipe. In such cases, we already know that the dependencies of such recipes are already built and available to us. We can use the -b option to build only that specific recipe and save our precious time.

> Do not use the -b option when you are unsure of dependencies

ContinuContinuing build even in the case of errors (-k, --continue)

The default behavior of BitBake is to stop on error after showing the logs where the error has occurred. However, if we run BitBake with this option, it would try to run as many tasks as possible. This option can be useful when we are building images with a lot of packages and we are not sure of errors. In such cases, we will have to build with some of the failures which we can fix, and invoke our build again. In failure cases target/recipe which encountered error and those which require it won't build,, yet BitBake will continue building instead of giving error and exiting. After the completion of the build we can fix the errors and rebuild.

Force-specific tasks (-f, --force)

BitBake builds tasks incrementally, and it has a mechanism of keeping stamps to ensure this. We need to bypass this mechanism in cases where we know that a specific task needs to be rebuilt. Such a scenario can be handled using the -f option. This option tells BitBake to ignore the stamps and run the specific task for that target, without considering whether it is already run or not; for example, if we execute the compile task, know that it is already run, and want to make sure it is re-executed. We can run the following command:

```
$ bitbake -c compile <package_name> -f
```

If we do this, the compile task will rerun, ignoring the stamps.

Using alternate providers (-a, --tryaltconfigs)

We can use this option to avoid failure of some packages using different providers. Examples of such recipes are kernel and uboot recipes. In the case of kernel, we will have multiple recipes providing our required target, which is virtual/kernel.

Executing a specific task (-c)

This is a very useful option and developers need it a lot. The BitBake recipe consists of multiple tasks; we will discuss them in detail. For now, we should know that a recipe consists of multiple functional units called **tasks**. Each of these is responsible for some functionality, such as fetching source code, configuring it, compiling it, and so on. It is more like targets in the case of Make, if you are familiar with it. We can tell BitBake to perform one of these. For example, while developing a recipe for some package, we have applied some changes in the source code and we want to verify that the fixes we applied are actually working. We need to just compile the code. In this case, we will use the following command:

```
$ bitbake -c compile <recipe name>
```

This command will not try to run tasks such as compile, fetch, unpack, and so on, if they are already run. There is one very useful task called `listtask` that can be used for experimentation. Later, we can use this task to gather information about available recipes. Try executing the following command in your build directory. Do not worry about its output if it looks weird, until we discuss tasks in detail in the next chapter.

```
$ bitbake -c listtasks procps
```

Invalidate stamps (-C, --clear-stamp)

This option tells BitBake to invalidate a stamp for a specified task, and then run the default build task. It is useful in cases where we are sure of our fix in some specific task, and we want to run all the remaining tasks of this package. For example, when we encountered some error in the configure task of a recipe, we fixed it. Now, we want all our tasks that are available for the package to be run. If we use -c, we would use the following combination of commands:

```
$ bitbake -c compile busybox
$ bitbake busybox
In case we are using -C, we will use
$ bitbake -C compile busybox
```

These commands will save us waiting time for the completion of the first command, and we can execute the second one manually.

Increasing verbosity (-v, --verbose)

General command increases the log message level of BitBake. Log message data is sent to the terminal.

Debug level (-D, --debug)

This command increases the debug level. It can be specified more than once. For example - DDD will flood your terminal with logs and debugging information. You may regret turning it on and learn some better ways of debugging. It is very useful for learning purposes. You can actually see what BitBake is doing.

Dry run (-n, --dry-run)

Don't actually execute anything, just walk through the metadata.

Parse only (-p, --parse-only)

Just parse BitBake and exit it. Do not start the next step of building packages.

Show versions (-s, --show-versions)

This option displays the preferred versions of all recipes. You can use grep on it to know about the specific package that version is actually building, in your case.

Get environment (-e, --environment)

This is a very useful option. This is a kind of Swiss army knife in your Yocto Project / BitBake toolbox, while working with recipes. You always need to know what is actually happening and which variable is getting what value. This option will help you know these details. You can redirect the output of this option to some file, and then get your required information from that file using the grep utility or your favorite text editor. One simple scenario that we can discuss here is knowing the value of the SRC_URI variable. In cases where we are assigning value in multiple files, we can determine the final value that is assigned to it using environment. In such cases, we will do something like this:

```
$ bitbake -e busybox > busybox.txt
```

Now, we can use the following command to get the value:

```
$ grep SRC_URI= busybox.txt
```

You will get output similar to the following one:

```
SRC_URI="http://www.busybox.net/downloads/busybox-1.22.1.tar.
bz2;name=tarball              file://get_header_tar.patch
file://busybox-appletlib-dependency.patch          file://busybox-
udhcpc-no_deconfig.patch          file://find-touchscreen.sh
file://busybox-cron          file://busybox-httpd          file://
busybox-udhcpd          file://default.script          file://
simple.script          file://hwclock.sh          file://mount.
busybox          file://syslog          file://syslog-startup.
conf          file://syslog.conf          file://busybox-
syslog.default          file://mdev          file://mdev.conf
file://umount.busybox          file://defconfig          file://
busybox-syslog.service.in          file://busybox-klogd.service.
in          file://fail_on_no_media.patch          file://
run-ptest          file://inetd.conf          file://inetd
file://login-utilities.cfg          file://0001-build-system-
Specify-nostldlib-when-linking-to-.o-fi.patch "
```

This assignment contains a number of files assigned to SRC_URI. These files might not have been assigned to it by a single use or, in some cases, not even by the same company. To know how this happens, just wait for the following chapters where we will discuss bbappends and layers.

While searching for a variable in an environment, append = with it to get the final value assigned to it.

Generating a dependency graph (-g, --graphviz)

Using this option, we can generate dependency information of our target. This information is stored using the dot syntax in .dot files. We can use these dot files to generate graph files as well. We can directly use these dot files to save time in generating graphs and concentrate on the investigation of the issue in hand. This should be used with the -I option to exclude recursive dependencies. For example, we want to generate a dependency tree for our core-image-minimal image. We can do this using the following command:

```
$ bitbake -g -I glib -I dbus -I busybox -I zlib core-image-minimal
```

This will generate four files, as shown in the following output, which is self-explanatory:

```
NOTE: PN build list saved to 'pn-buildlist'
NOTE: PN dependencies saved to 'pn-depends.dot'
NOTE: Package dependencies saved to 'package-depends.dot'
NOTE: Task dependencies saved to 'task-depends.dot'
```

In the preceding command, we are suppressing the recursive dependencies for GLib, dbus, and BusyBox.

Log levels (-l DEBUG_DOMAINS, --log-domains=DEBUG_DOMAINS)

We can set the log level using this option to save logs on the disk, according to our requirements.

Profile (-P, --profile)

This option profiles the command and saves the output in the build directory.

Select UI (-u UI, --ui=UI)

You can use the UI type using this option. The available values for UI are knotty, hob, and depexp.

Don't use shared state (--no-setscene)

Turn off using feature shared state. BitBake keeps trying to avoid rebuilding packages that are already built. They are kept in the shared state. This option tells BitBake not to use packages kept in the shared state, but to build everything from scratch.

Summary

In this chapter, we discussed a brief history of BitBake. You learned the goals and problem areas that BitBake has considered, thus making itself a unique option for Embedded Linux Development. You also learned how BitBake actually works. Finally, we went through different options of BitBake, using examples to illustrate the important ones.

In the next chapter, you will learn how to create a basic hello world recipe and discuss its different elements.

3
Creating the helloworld Recipe

In the previous chapter, you learned the history of BitBake, its options, and how it works. In this chapter, we will create our first demo application, a very basic one, helloworld demo. Creating and running such an application does not require much effort. In this chapter, we will:

- Learn the basic elements of a recipe
- Learn the contents of work and build directory
- Have an overview of tasks
- Learn how to deploy packages

Creating helloworld

Yocto Project provides us with helping scripts to ease our tasks. You will learn some of these scripts during the course of this book. To create our helloworld recipe, we will use one such script, called `yocto-layer`. This script can be found under the scripts directory in poky. Primarily, this script is meant to create a layer that is used to arrange various sets of recipes. Currently, if we have a look at the contents of our poky directory, which we created in first chapter for creation of images, we have the following directories. These directories are layers, as can be found using the `find` command:

```
$ find . -name layer.conf
./meta/conf/layer.conf
./meta-skeleton/conf/layer.conf
./meta-yocto-bsp/conf/layer.conf
./meta-yocto/conf/layer.conf
./meta-selftest/conf/layer.conf
```

All of these are Poky layers, and we cannot use any of these to keep our metadata. Technically, this is not impossible, but it is not a recommended way of development. So, we will create our own layer using the preceding script. While doing this, we will ask the script to create an example recipe for us as well. How simple! Let's look at the following command sequence:

```
[irfan@pkl-irfan-ubuntu]$ scripts/yocto-layer create ybdevelop
Please enter the layer priority you'd like to use for the layer: [default: 6]
Would you like to have an example recipe created? (y/n) [default: n] y
Please enter the name you'd like to use for your example recipe: [default: example] helloworld
Would you like to have an example bbappend file created? (y/n) [default: n]

New layer created in meta-ybdevelop.

Don't forget to add it to your BBLAYERS (for details see meta-ybdevelop\README).
```

Yocto Project layer script invocation

As you can see, in the preceding sequence, we are presented with four options in total. We choose the first and last as defaults. The second option we choose is y to create an example recipe, which, in turn, requires us to provide the name `helloworld` for the recipe we want to create.

To enable this layer, we need to add its path to `bblayers.conf` in our `build_bbb/conf` . In our case, it looks as follows:

```
BBLAYERS ?= " \
  /home/irfan/yocto/poky/meta \
  /home/irfan/yocto/poky/meta-yocto \
  /home/irfan/yocto/poky/meta-yocto-bsp \
  /home/irfan/yocto/poky/meta-ybdevelop \
"

BBLAYERS_NON_REMOVABLE ?= " \
  /home/irfan/yocto/poky/meta \
  /home/irfan/yocto/poky/meta-yocto \
"
```

This script created the directory structure, as shown in preceding screenshot, but we will change it a little bit for our convenience in future. We will rename the directory example `helloworld` so that we can unambiguously use the `recipes-example` directory for our other examples as well. Contents created by this command are shown in the following screenshot. For this chapter, we will be interested in the marked rectangular region that is our recipe helloworld. We will leave the rest of the discussions, which are related to layers, for the upcoming chapters. So, in the rest of the chapter, we will work mostly with the following files:

- `helloworld_0.1.bb`
- `helloworld.c`
- `example.patch`

The first one is the base file. We have been using the word recipe for so long. Here, for our `helloworld` file, `helloworld_0.1.bb` is the recipe. Let's have a look at what this file contains and what the various lines in it mean:

```
[irfan@pkl-irfan-ubuntu]$  tree meta-ybdevelop/
meta-ybdevelop/
├── conf
│   └── layer.conf
├── COPYING.MIT
├── README
└── recipes-example
    └── example
        ├── helloworld-0.1
        │   ├── example.patch
        │   └── helloworld.c
        └── helloworld_0.1.bb

4 directories, 6 files
```

Layer contents

Contents of the helloworld recipe

A recipe file is actually a set of instructions/actions that BitBake will perform, for our package to be created. This name is inspired by a cooking recipe, as BitBake itself is inspired from the cooking terminology, baking. In our case, it is `helloworld_0.1.bb`. Let's walk through the contents of the `helloworld_0.1.bb` recipe:

- The top of this file contains comments about its derivation, since it is derived from the Yocto Project documentation.

- `DESCRIPTION`: This variable contains a string value. For any recipe we can and should provide a description to let the users know what this recipe is about.

- `SECTION`: In this variable, we define what type of recipe it is. In our case, it is an example. In other cases, it can be utilities, graphics, kernel, and so on.

- `LICENSE`: Here, we specify the type of license we want to use for our recipe. In our case, it is MIT. Other values can be BSD, GPL, or your custom license. However, you need to provide a license file for your selected license in the next variable.

- `LIC_FILES_CHKSUM`: We need to provide a license file along with its `md5 sum` command. Here, we will use the MIT license file from a common collection of licenses. This collection is found under `poky` in `meta/files/common-licenses/`. You can get the file's MD5 Sum using the `md5sum` command as follows:

```
$ md5sum meta/files/common-licenses/MIT
0835ade698e0bcf8506ecda2f7b4f302  meta/files/common-licenses/MIT
```

You can verify that it is the same as its set.

 Failing to provide the correct MD5 Sum for the license file will trigger build errors. A good thing about this error is that BitBake suggests the correct value as well, that we can use as it is, in most cases.

- `PR`: This is a package that is a `helloworld` revision. We are setting it to `r0` in this case, which is the default assignment. We can override its value in our recipe.

- `SRC_URI`: In this variable, we specify what sources we want to build. In our case, we want to build `helloworld.c`. The source file is on the disk in the directory named `helloworld-0.1`. This directory is similar to our recipe name, with one minute difference of – and _, and of course, there is no `.bb` postfix. All files from such a directory are accessible to `SRC_URI`.

- s: Here, we specify the source directory, where we can do all the building and expect sources to be placed there. In our case, we are setting it to WORKDIR. For now, remember this; we will see how this expands, to what values, and where these are actually created, in a while.

- do_compile: This is a BitBake task. We are overriding the default task and supplying our own command for compilation here. We are invoking the compiler to compile helloworld.c into a helloworld binary.

- do_install: This is another BitBake task. We are again overriding the default behavior and supplying our own commands. In the first command, we are creating a directory, under the path to which variable D points. The directory created at this location will be as set in the bindir variable, which is in /usr/bin. In the next command, we will copy the helloworld binary created earlier to the directory created just now.

Recipe naming and related variables

Recipes are named using the following convention:

```
<package>_<version>.bb
```

This in turn translates into two variables, namely, PN and PV. PN stands for Package Name, and PV stands for Package Version. These variables are available in our recipes and are extensively used for various manipulations. For example, PN is added to PROVIDES, and BitBake builds everything that is present in PROVIDES. In this case, we are not explicitly specifying the value of PROVIDES anywhere. That's why it is set to PN. In another case, it will be set to the value we set.

Building a recipe

Now that we have created a recipe, we are ready to build it. We already know how to build a recipe by invoking the simple BitBake <recipename> command as follows in our specific case:

```
$ bitbake helloworld
```

Do not forget to set an environment before running BitBake commands. You can set the environment by running the following command:
```
$ source oe-init-build-env build_bbb
```

We are omitting the output of this command for brevity. This will build our helloworld application/package/recipe. Thus, the binary helloworld that is created can be found at tmp/work/cortexa8hf-vfp-neon-poky-linux-gnueabi/helloworld/0.1-r0/helloworld. How can we know where some specific package will be found? Do we need to run a find command for this, or is there some criterion followed? Yes, we have a certain criteria followed here. For this, we need to look into how the WORKDIR variable is constructed. If we grep this variable from bitbake.conf, which can be found under poky/meta/conf/ directory, we get the following:

```
WORKDIR = "${BASE_WORKDIR}/${MULTIMACH_TARGET_SYS}/
${PN}/${EXTENDPE}${PV}-${PR}"
```

So, understanding the meaning of these constituent variables resolves the dilemma:

- BASE_WORKDIR: This is defined in the ${TMPDIR}/work directory.

- TMPDIR: This is the directory named tmp under our build directory, which is build_bbb.

- MULTIMACH_TARGET_SYS: This is the target system identifier. In our case it resolves to cortexa8hf-vfp-neon-poky-linux-gnueabi. This is set according to the tune file used in machine.conf.

- PN: This is our package name, which is helloworld.

- EXTENDPE: The epoch, empty in our case. We will worry about it when we set it.

- PV: This is our package version, which is 0.1. So, our next directory is prefixed with it.

- PR: This is our package revision. We set it to r0.

Try changing PR = "r1" in the recipe and rerun BitBake helloworld. Then, visit tmp/work/ cortexa8hf-vfp-neon-poky-linux-gnueabi/helloworld. You will notice that a new directory, 0.1-r1, is created. Similarly, you can play with PR and PN and observe the differences. These are updated when the recipe is updated. BitBake takes care of it for us.

Build directories

Let's have a quick look at the WORKDIR directory. Most of these directories are created and populated when the related task is executed. To have a look at it, let's execute the following command:

```
$ tree tmp/work/cortexa8hf-vfp-neon-poky-linux-gnueabi/helloworld/0.1-r0/
-dL 1
```

Here is the output of this command:

```
tmp/work/cortexa8hf-vfp-neon-poky-linux-gnueabi/helloworld/0.1-r0/
├── deploy-ipks
├── image
├── license-destdir
├── package
├── packages-split
├── patches
├── pkgdata
├── pseudo
├── sysroot-destdir
└── temp
```

Let's go through these by giving a short description of each:

- deploy-ipks: The final package (ipk in our case) is placed in this directory.

- image: Image contents go into this directory. The Do_install task installs contents to this directory before they are added to the respective packages.

- license-destdir: License-related information is contained in this directory.

- package: This is a shared place that contains package data when it is being generated, during the process of package creation.

- packages-split: Different types of packages are separated, and their relevant data is placed under this directory.

- patches: This contains symbolic links to patches.

- pkgdata: This directory contains package data before they are split.

- pseudo: DB for BitBake use pseudo for speeding up the process.

- sysroot-destdir: This allows contents to be copied to the sysroot directory under tmp.

- temp: All the scripts for tasks are created in this directory with PID, along with logfiles for each task.

Tasks

This topic is long due. In the previous chapters we discussed tasks, but not in much detail. Tasks can be considered as units of execution to perform a specific function, or a set of related functions that can be combined together. The `helloword` tasks can be listed using the `-c listtasks` option of BitBake:

```
$ bitbake -c listtasks helloworld
```

Even for this basic recipe list, there are more than 20 tasks. In this output, each task contains a short description of it, which should be consulted first. We are skipping the list for brevity. Most of the tasks are not seen in the recipes. Why? We are content with the default implementations provided to us, which are automatically used if we do not want to override them. All these tasks are prefixed by `do_`. Here, we will discuss the most common tasks, to develop our understanding of them.

Build

This is like a placeholder task, to tell bitbake when we do not provide a specific task to be run. We don't have to tell bitbake to run this specific task. We simply mention `none` and it is picked. Now, we will look at other tasks in the logical sequence of execution.

> To develop a better understanding of the upcoming tasks, you should execute each with the `-c` option of BitBake and analyze the contents of the corresponding directories.

Fetch

First of all, we need to get the sources for the package[s] we want to build. The `do_fetch` task is responsible for performing this operation. We have seen the `SRC_URI` variable in our recipe. This task will use this variable to know where to get the source code. In our case, we are telling it to get the `helloworld.c` file from disk, as we are using the `file://` protocol. By the end of this task, all the content specified in `SRC_URI` is made available in `DL_DIR`, that is, the `downloads` directory, which we covered in the first chapter. To develop an understanding of what is actually happening, we should run BitBake `-c fetch helloworld` and then look for new files created in this directory.

Unpack

The next stage is to place the contents from the `download` directory in the `${PV}-${PR}` (`0.1-r0`) directory:

```
"${BASE_WORKDIR}/${MULTIMACH_TARGET_SYS}/${PN}/${EXTENDPE}${PV}-${PR}"
```

In our specific case, it is `tmp/work/ cortexa8hf-vfp-neon-poky-linux-gnueabi/ helloworld/0.1-r0/`. This directory now contains the `helloworld.c` file in it.

Patch

If we have specified some patches in `SRC_URI`, then we get all these patches placed under `${PV}-${PR}/` at the completion of the `do_unpack` task. In this task, these patches are applied to our source code. For `helloworld`, you can create a patch to change the output line in our example and see what happens. Make it print **Hello World! Patched**.

Configure

This task is responsible for the configuration steps required for the packages to be built. BitBake provides us with the default implementation of this as well, which we can use to ease our development process. Our recipe is a simple one and doesn't need such a task. However, if we have some autotools (helloworld has `configure. ac` available), then we can use inherit autotools in our recipe, and skip the rest of the recipe. You may want to override the default settings in this case as well, for example, supplying extra configuration using `EXTR_OECONF`. Here's the command for the configuration:

```
EXTRA_OECONF += "--enable-something"
```

We will see more examples of its use in advanced recipes.

Compile

We are overriding this task in our recipe. If we had created a Makefile, we could have used something such as `oe_runmake`. For the autotools recipe, we might not need to override this task. We can provide extra arguments using `EXTRA_OEMAKE` just like we did in the case of configure. The default for this is to run make utility. Compilation takes place in the directory pointed by `B`. This is the same as `S` and we have made `S` equals to `WORKDIR`.

Install

This is also created by us in our recipe. This task basically runs make install if the make file is available. Thus, the compiled contents are copied to the directory pointed by the D variable. D is pointing to the image folder discussed earlier.

Package

This task performs an analysis of data placed in the directory pointed to by the D variable, which is the image folder. Then, it is copied to the packages folder. Based on the analysis, it places data into the corresponding directory for package type, under the package-split directory. For example, in our case, if we look at the contents of the packages-split directory, two package types are populated: helloworld and helloworld-dbg.

The package_write_<package> statement creates packages depending on the type(s) selected. In our case, it writes ipks and placing them under deploy-ipks/cortexa8hf-vfp-neon/.

The listtasks utility task lists the tasks in a recipe, when used with the -c option of BitBake.

Devshell

This is a useful task to debug our recipes during the development process. We can launch our recipe in a separate shell and get the environment already set for us. We can start experimenting and observing what's going wrong.

Clean

This task is also a utility task and is available for all recipes. It removes the output of all tasks that are performed after unpacking.

Cleansstate

The do_clean + function removes shared state data.

The following command will clean the state of particular packages:

```
Bitbake -c cleansstate libusb
```

Cleaning the state of packages would be helpful if your system faces unexpected failure due to power, or some other reasons, when compilation of a particular task is going on.

After resuming, the compilation may go through errors of that particular package, due to the error state of that package. It is hard to trace the errors out.

This command will solve this issue

Cleanall

The `do_cleansstate` + function removes downloaded data as well from `DL_DIR`.

Overriding default tasks

We can override the default tasks by providing an empty implementation, as follows:

```
do_<taskname>() {
   :
}
```

Deploying helloworld

We are dealing with embedded systems and creating a package for an embedded board, that is, BeagleBone. Preparing a package alone doesn't make sense. We cannot run it on the host system. So, the next logical step is to actually deploy our package onto an embedded board. For such a simple recipe, we could have used simple compilation steps, copied the binary on our board and ran it. However, such a technique would have become a nightmare in a simple BSP, where we may easily have to do this for more than 1000 packages. Hence, we are using Yocto Project. We have the following two ways to deploy any recipe.

Manually installing a package

We can manually copy our package from `tmp/deploy/ipk/cortexa8hf-vfp-neon/` `helloworld_0.1-r0_cortexa8hf-vfp-neon.ipk` to our board using SCP over SSH, or any other technique available. We can copy it to an SD card and install it on the board, using the following command:

```
# opkg install  helloworld_0.1-r0_cortexa8hf-vfp-neon.ipk
```

This is not a very clean/systematic way of doing things. It should be used in cases where we are dealing with a small number of packages, or where we are performing some experimentation.

Making an image dependent on our package

To do this, we need to add `helloworld` to `CORE_EXTRA_IMAGE_INSTALL` in our `local.conf` or `auto.conf` file as follows:

```
CORE_EXTRA_IMAGE_INSTALL += "helloworld"
```

We need to build the `core-image-sato` image:

```
$ bitbake core-image-sato
```

This will build our image as part of helloworld, and install it at its desired location.

Summary

In this chapter, we created a `helloworld` recipe using the Yocto Project script for layer creation. We modified it a little bit to suit our needs and explained various elements contained in the recipe. We built the recipe and viewed the changes made in the directory structure. Finally, you learned how to deploy it to a target.

In the next chapter, you will learn about complex recipes, taking examples from GStreamer to add multimedia to our system.

4
Adding Multimedia to Your Board

In the previous chapter, we created a `helloworld` recipe and learned the basic elements of a BitBake recipe related to it. In this chapter, we will study a more complex set of recipes related to multimedia. We won't create a recipe of our own. Instead, we will examine a player called **gaku**, that is already available. Fortunately, this is all set in the image we built in our first chapter, `core-image-sato`. We will see how this is enabled for this specific image type and how we can enable such a package in any other image. While doing this, we will cover the advanced elements of BitBake recipes.

In this chapter, we will cover the following topics:

- Introducing gaku
- Recipe of gaku
- GStreamer recipes short trip
- Action time

Introducing gaku

Gaku is a simple music player to play music. It uses GTK+ as the user interface library and GStreamer as a multimedia framework. Since we are building `core-image-sato` from *Chapter 1, Welcome to Yocto Project and BeagleBone Black*, we already have this added to our image, and we don't have to do anything extra to enable it. Here, we will use a top-to-bottom approach to learn how this is enabled, and what packages it depends on.

Hence, we will start analyzing the player recipe and from there, we will dig its dependencies and have a look at the required recipes. We will look at GStreamer recipes as well. Meanwhile, we will encounter different BitBake elements and syntax-specific discussions.

In summary, in the case of `core-image-sato`, multimedia is enabled by adding gaku to image dependencies using the package group `packagegroup-core-x11-sato.bb`. This package, in turn, causes the rest of the dependencies to be fulfilled and built with it. This package is found at `meta/recipes-sato/packagegroups/packagegroup-core-x11-sato.bb`.

Line 57 of this file is adding the player. We will discuss package groups in detail in the next chapter, which is dedicated to layers.

The recipe for gaku

The recipe for gaku can be found at `meta/recipes-sato/gaku/gaku_git.bb`. We have already discussed most of the elements. We will discuss only those that we haven't already discussed, or that need some more explanation. We will discuss the contents of the recipe, as well as the other options similar to the ones used, and not used, in the content.

Package control variables

In this section, we will discuss the variables that are used to control a package. Three of the variables belonging to this type are found in our recipe; the rest are not. We will discuss those as well.

Build dependencies (DEPENDS)

We already informed you that gaku uses GTK+ for UI and GStreamer as a multimedia framework. It sets its dependency on these, as follows:

```
DEPENDS = "gtk+ gstreamer libowl-av"
```

`libowl-av` is a widget library that provides widgets for video and audio playback, thus easing the creation of multimedia applications. Moreover, these widgets are integrated with GStreamer.

 Talking in terms of tasks, this makes `do_configure` dependent on `do_populate_sysroot` of the one it depends on.

Runtime dependencies (RDEPENDS)

If runtime dependencies packages are not available in the root file system, our package won't be able to run. These runtime dependencies are provided using `RDEPENDS_${PN}`. This mechanism is called package name override. Thus, this runtime dependency is set on a specific package. This kind of syntax could have been avoided in Yocto Project releases prior to 1.4, but now, it is mandatory:

```
RDEPENDS_${PN} = "gst-plugins-base-audioconvert \
            gst-plugins-base-audioresample \
            gst-plugins-base-typefindfunctions \
            gst-plugins-base-playbin"
```

As you might have noticed, these packages contain `base`, since these are related to the GStreamer base set of plugins. If you try to locate these packages under meta, you won't be successful. GStreamer is a big set of recipes using complex constructs; that's why we chose it.

 Talking in terms of tasks, `do_build` of our package is dependent on `do_package_write_ipk` of the listed ones.

Runtime recommendations (RRECOMMENDS)

These packages are required for extra functionalities. If we skip these packages, we won't get any runtime dependency errors. However, the functionality will certainly not be available, which is provided by these:

```
RRECOMMENDS_${PN} = "gst-plugins-good-id3demux \
            gst-plugins-base-vorbis \
            gst-plugins-base-alsa \
            gst-plugins-base-ogg \
            ${COMMERCIAL_AUDIO_PLUGINS}"
```

`COMMERCIAL_AUDIO_PLUGINS` is a variable that we need to provide, using the `local.conf` file, which we discussed in *Chapter 1*, *Welcome to Yocto Project and BeagleBone Black*. If we don't need any of the commercial audio plugins, we don't need to worry about them. However, if we care about commercial formats, such as MP3, then we need to enable them. These plugins will require us to white list licenses for commercial format as well; otherwise, we will hit errors.

We will use the following code in our case in `local.conf` to accomplish both of these plugins:

```
LICENSE_FLAGS_WHITELIST = "commercial"
COMMERCIAL_AUDIO_PLUGINS = "gst-plugins-ugly-mad \
         gst-plugins-ugly-mpegaudioparse"
```

In the first line, we are white listing commercial licenses, while in the second, we are enabling plugins for mad and MPEG formats. Using this process of white listing, we are telling BitBake not to issue or give error for packages; here GStreamer ugly plugins, which has commercial licenses will cause error otherwise.

Now, let's discuss some of the package-controlling variables that are not present in our recipe under consideration, but we need to know about them.

RCONFLICTS

This variable can be used to specify the conflicting packages without package. For example, when we are using some graphical server other than X11, say wayland, and we are not supporting X11, we can use something like this:

```
RCONFLICTS_${PN} = "x11"
```

RREPLACE

If our package is replacing a package or a set of packages, we can use this package-controlling variable to specify this. The other package or packages will be removed on the installation of our package:

```
RREPLACES_${PN} = "package (1.0)"
```

PROVIDES

The default value for this is the package name. However, there can be cases where we explicitly want to specify what our recipe is providing. In such cases, we can use this variable. For example, kernel recipes provide virtual/kernel, and in our machine configuration file, we specify which recipe is to be used. We can add only those values to DEPENDS that are already added to PROVIDES, of any recipes. The default value for PROVIDES comes from `bitbake.conf` as follows:

```
PROVIDES_prepend = "${PN} "
```

Don't worry about prepend; we will discuss it shortly.

RPROVIDES

This is used to explicitly specify what is provided by a package at runtime. Just like PROVIDES, a package name is already in the RPROVIDES list. We need to only specify otherwise. This is used to satisfy RDEPENDS for other packages.

Source control in a recipe

In this section, we will discuss variables and syntaxes related to source control of a package. We already discussed it a little bit in *Chapter 3, Creating the helloworld Recipe*, but there, we discussed only an elementary-type file:// protocol. In this recipe, luckily, we have the git:// type, which is more advanced. Understanding it will make it easier for us to play with any other type. Here are the lines related to source control in our recipe:

```
SRCREV = "a0be2fe4b5f12b8b07f4e3bd624b3729657f0ac5"
PV = "0.1+git${SRCPV}"
SRC_URI = "git://git.yoctoproject.org/${BPN}"
S = "${WORKDIR}/git"
```

SRCREV

Here, we are specifying the commit hash to be used for our build. We can also specify to check out from the latest available hash, using the following syntax:

```
SRCREV = "${AUTOREV}"
```

PV calculation

Since we can choose to get the latest code of the package from the Git repository, if we use hardcoded value for PV, it would be difficult to know what revision it was built for. So, we have a mechanism of SRCPV used to get the source revision. It is defined in meta/conf/bitbake.conf as follows:

```
SRCPV = "${@bb.fetch2.get_srcrev(d)}"
```

Thus, our PV calculation statement results in 0.1+gitAUTOINC+a0be2fe4b5, where a0be2fe4b5 is the short hash that we set in our recipe.

Change SRCREV to AUTOREV as follows:

```
SRCREV = "a0be2fe4b5f12b8b07f4e3bd624b3729657f0ac5" to
SRCREV = "${AUTOREV}"
```

Then, rebuild using the following code:

```
bitbake -C cleansstate gaku
```

Observe the difference by checking what new ${WORKDIR} value is named to.

The SRC_URI specification

Here, the following line specifies the source URI:

```
SRC_URI = "git://git.yoctoproject.org/${BPN}"
```

Since the URI is starting with git://, BitBake knows it is Git repository, and it should be using the Git protocol.

We can also use the local Git repository using the following syntax:

```
SRC_URI = "file:///path/to/path;protocol=file"
```

Also, we can use the https protocol using the following syntax:

```
SRC_URI = "https://git.yoctoproject.org/${BPN}"
```

Further, we can specify a branch using the branch=master syntax, which is separated using similar syntax as that of the file protocol.

Also, we know about PN but not about BPN yet. BPN is not much different form PN. We can have multiple versions of recipes, such as -native and -cross. In such cases, recipes are named BPN-native_${PV}.bb, so BPN is computed by stripping these extra suffixes from PN. In our case, both PN and BPN are same, as can be seen by looking at the environment that is running the following command:

```
$ bitbake -e gaku > env.txt
```

This environment also runs the grep command:

```
$ grep "PN=" env-gaku.txt
PN="gaku"
BPN="gaku"
```

The S directory

Here, we are using only the `git://` protocol. In this case, a directory named Git will be created under `${WORKDIR}`, and all of the sources from the repository will be unpacked under this directory. Hence, we are setting `S` to point to this directory:

```
S = "${WORKDIR}/git"
```

Inheriting classes

We are inheriting two classes here to ease our task of compilation. These are `autotools` and `pkgconfig`, as we can see in the last line of the recipe:

```
inherit autotools pkgconfig
```

This avoids much of the hustle for configuration and compilation. We are using default configure and compile in this case.

First, `autotools` tells us to use `autotools.bbclass`. This class takes care of the configure, compile, and install tasks. We don't need to worry about them. The later one, `pkgconfig`, is adding `pkgconfig.bbclass` and provides a standard way of getting header and library information.

> If you are using USB headphones, you might have to enable kernel configuration related to it, which is not enabled by default. For this, you need to use the following command:
>
> **$ bitbake -c menuconfig virtual/kernel**
>
> It will open a new terminal for kernel configurations.

GStreamer recipes' short trip

This section is not intended for a full walkthrough of GStreamer, its recipes, and other information required to grasp multimedia application development using GStreamer. Instead, we intend to have a look at different recipes, find BitBake elements in them, and discuss those elements. If we observe the order as we encountered in the gaku recipe, first of all, we set GStreamer in DEPENDS. Here are the main recipes for GStreamer:

- `gstreamer_0.10.36.bb`
- `gst-plugins-base_0.10.36.bb`

- `gst-meta-base_0.10.bb`
- `gst-plugins-package.inc`
- `gst-plugins.inc`

These can be found under `meta/recipes-multimedia/gstreamer/`. We don't have the luxury of enough pages to go into the details of each of these, and the relationships of each with the other. Hence, we will discuss the common constructs found in these files.

Types of variable assignments

Having a look at this recipe, we encounter "`?=`", "`+=`", and "`??=`". We recommend that you read this chapter for details. We will discuss them here but in brief.

- `=`: This is a simple variable assignment. It requires `""` and spaces are significant.

- `?=`: This is used to assign a default value to a variable. It can be overridden using `=`.

- `??=`: This is a weak default value assignment. This is similar to `?=`, but it is done at the end of the parsing process. If multiple `??=` are used, only the last one is picked.

- `:=`: This is an immediate variable expansion. The value thus assigned is expanded immediately.

- `+=`: This appends a value to a variable with space.

- `=+`: This prepends a value to a variable with space.

- `.=`: This is a kind of string concatenation. This appends a value to a variable without any space.

- `=.`: This prepends a value without space.

- `_append`: This is the same as `.=` but more readable and widely used. Also, keep in mind that it is not an immediate assignment. You need to remember for precedence.

- `_prepend`: This is the same as `=`, but more readable and widely used. Also, keep in mind, that it is not an immediate assignment. You need to remember for precedence.

- `_remove`: This causes all occurrences of values from a variable to be removed.

Never underestimate the chances of using the wrong type and facing issues.

EXTRA_OECONF

We find `EXTRA_OECONF` with a lot of value assignments. This is the input variable for the `autotools` class. All these are options of the configure script. If you are to run the configure script manually, you will be supplying these options to `./configure`. Here, this is done by the `autotools` class. Similarly, we have `EXTRA_OEMAKE`. Have a look at `poky/meta/classes/autotools.bbclass` to understand how these are appended, while executing the configure script.

The FILES_ variables

Also, we find the `FILES_` variables in this recipe. These variables are used to tell what files are to be packed in what package types. If we fail to pack some files to their respective package types and they are created, BitBake will give us warnings. Here, we are creating `default`, `dev`, `dbg`, `staticdev`, `apps`, and `glib` packages.

Variable flags

Also, we find the syntax of the `VAR[a]` type, for example, `PACKAGECONFIG[x11]` and `PACKAGECONFIG[orc]`. These are called **Variable Flags**. This mechanism enables us to `store/set/associate properties/attributes` to variables. We can use all the preceding operations. Only the style syntax (`_append`, `_prepend`, `_remove`) is not supported.

ALLOW_EMPTY

In short, to turn the recipes to functionality only, we use this:

```
ALLOW_EMPTY_${PN} = "1"
```

It tells BitBake to not package our recipe. Thus, a package is produced, even if no contents are added to it. This should always be used with `_${PN}`. To understand such a scenario, sometimes we need to create things that are not destined to be used in `rootfs` and hence, don't need packaging. DTB files generation can be an example of such a task, where we place the generated DTB file in the deploy directory. It doesn't make sense to create a package for it.

FILESPATH

We need to specify extra paths, if any, to be used to look for source files or patches. This is required only if we are supposed to place these in non-default paths as they are specified in `base.bbclass`, which is found in meta/classes, as follows:

```
FILESPATH = "${@base_set_filespath(["${FILE_DIRNAME}/${BP}",
"${FILE_DIRNAME}/${BPN}", "${FILE_DIRNAME}/files"], d)}"
        fpaths = (d.getVar('FILESPATH', True) or '').split(':')
```

We can also use the `FILESEXTRAPATHS` variable, but this should be used in combination with conditional syntax variables:

```
FILESEXTRAPATHS_append := ":${THISDIR}/extra_file"
FILESEXTRAPATHS_prepend := "${THISDIR}/extra_file:"
```

 Note that in the preceding lines of code, one statement has a colon while the other does not.

Conditional overriding mechanisms

BitBake has a mechanism of `OVERRIDES`, to control the values to be assigned to variables conditionally, depending on settings in configuration files. `OVERRIDES` is a colon-separated list. This is used if you are using a variable dependent on some architecture, say qemux86, and we have qemux86 in `OVERRIDES`. So, in our case, the following values will be assigned to the `RRECOMMENDS_${PN}` variable only when qemux86 is in overrides. This will be the case when we will build for qemux86:

```
RRECOMMENDS_${PN}_qemux86 += "kernel-module-snd-ens1370
kernel-module-snd-rawmidi"
RRECOMMENDS_${PN}_qemux86-64 += "kernel-module-snd-ens1370
kernel-module-snd-rawmidi"
```

These variables can also be used in combination with conditional flag syntaxes (_append, _prepends), so that values are appended to variables conditionally. This is not used in our recipes under discussion. As an example will be we have architecture-dependent files to be added to `SRC_URI` sources. In this case, we will use something like this:

```
SRC_URI_append_arm = "file:///armfile"
SRC_URI_append_qemux86 = "file:///qemux86"
```

Reusing and sharing the same code

We have used inherit in multiple recipes; this directive is used for class files. This can only be used in classes and recipes. The same functionality can be used in configuration files, as well as with another directive, called INHERIT. Its syntax is different; it is used with += as follows:

```
INHERIT += "rm_work"
```

We can specify this in our `local.conf` file. This will cause the word directory to be removed after the completion of the build process. We discussed it in the first chapter. Using this syntax will cause all of the recipes to inherit such functionality, which will not be the case of other syntaxes, which are used in recipes.

We have listed GStreamer-related recipe files earlier. Two of these files have the `.inc` extension. This is a way of using similar/common functionality across multiple recipes. We use two different directives to serve this purpose:

- Require
- Include

These directives cause the contents of a specified file to be inserted where it is specified. The only difference in the two, is the case of handling when a specified file is not there. In case of include, there is no error if the file is not found, but in the case of require, an error is thrown.

Action time

Now, we have developed an understanding of the underlying details. We have built images that contain a video player, that is, gaku and GStreamer, to support this player as a multimedia framework. We have enabled a minimal set of plugins for our use. Having all this, we are ready to see how this actually works. Perform the following steps to see this in action.

1. Connect your board with the HDMI display. I have used my Samsung 32" LED TV for this purpose.
2. To connect the TV to the board, I used a micro HDMI-to-HDMI cable.
3. Copy some `.ogg` video file. You can convert some existing video file. You can download video files from `http://techslides.com/sample-webm-ogg-and-mp4-video-files-for-html5`.

4. Copy your downloaded video file to the board, directly onto a card, or using SSH, if you have connected the board to a network.

5. Launch gaku from UI.

6. I attached a USB mouse to use the UI.

7. Use the **+** button to browse to the directory containing the `sample.ogg` file.

8. Choose your copied video file (in my case, `sample.ogg`) and play it.

I was able to view the video on my TV and listen to the sounds using USB headphones. You can try enabling/disabling more GStreamer plugins to play other formats as well. It should be fun.

Summary

In this chapter, we studied more advanced recipe elements using gaku, a player based on GStreamer. We visited its recipe, as well as common elements from `gstreamer` recipes. We discussed these:

- How dependencies are specified and how multiple recipes are kept to provide the same package
- Some more about source fetching
- Various techniques to inherit functionalities
- Variable assignment types and conditional assignments

In next chapter, we will be studying Layers, a mechanism to keep all of our recipes together.

5
Creating and Exploring Layers

In this chapter, we will discuss layers, a powerful mechanism for the organization and reuse of metadata. We will also discuss the creation of layers using the script `yocto-layer`. Then, we will move on to various configuration options to organize the metadata and types of layers. We will cover aiding techniques of append files usage and `packagegroups`. We will discuss image customization as well.

Layer creation using script

We should always start with something easy, in order to keep things simple. So, a simple way to create a layer is to execute the following command from the script directory, under the `poky` directory:

```
$ ./scripts/yocto-layer create test
```

This will create a directory named `meta-test` in the `poky` directory, from where we invoke this command. However, before that, you have to answer some questions. The answers are discussed in these steps:

- Enter the layer priority you'd like to use for this layer: [default: 6] 7
- Check whether you would like to have an example recipe created: (y/n) [default: n]
- Check whether you would you like to have an example `bbappend` file created: (y/n) [default: n] y

- Enter the name you'd like to use for your bbappend file: [default: example]
  `helloworld`

- Enter the version number you'd like to use for your bbappend file,
  (this should match the recipe you're appending the file to): [default: 0.1]

Then, this script will notify us about enabling our newly created layer, which we need to remember. We can postpone this till we start building packages or images.

> Don't forget to add this layer to your BBLAYERS
> (for details, refer to `meta-test\READ`.

So, without ignoring this, we add this to our `conf/bblayers.conf` file at the end of the experimentation.

Now, let's take a look at what the script has created for us in the `meta-test` directory. The following is the output of the tree command:

```
$  tree meta-test/
meta-test/
├── conf
│   └── layer.conf
├── COPYING.MIT
├── README
└── recipes-example-bbappend
    └── example-bbappend
        ├── helloworld-0.1
        │   └── example.patch
        └── helloworld_0.1.bbappend
```

Let's perform some experimentation steps on this newly created layer before having discussions, such as what content we have in this directory, what it means, and so on. Let's do something practical first, and then we will dig into the details.

Patch in our Git source from the latest commit, which can be created using the following steps:

1. Modify the source file/files.

2. Commit these changes: `git add *` and `git commit -m "Custom patch"`.

3. Executing the patch as `git format-patch -n HEAD^` will give you the output as `001-Custom patch.patch`.

4. Rename the `example.patch` file to `print.patch`.

5. Add the following code to it:

```
+++ helloworld.c
--- ../helloworld.c
@@ -2,7 +2,7 @@
 int main(int argc, char **argv)
 {
-    printf("Hello World!\n");
+    printf("Hello World! Patched from bbappend !\n");

     return 0;
 }
```

6. Save it.

7. Open the `helloworld_0.1.bbappend` file.

8. Remove everything from it, accept the first line, and add the following line to it:

```
SRC_URI_append = " file://print.patch"
```

9. The total content of this file will now look like this:

```
FILESEXTRAPATHS_prepend := "${THISDIR}/${PN}-${PV}:"

SRC_URI_append = " file://print.patch"
```

10. Run the following command to clean up previous build contents:

```
$ bitbake -c cleansstate helloworld
```

Run the following command to build till the patching task:

```
$ bitbake -c patch helloworld
```

11. Take a look at the `helloworld.c` file from `${WORKDIR}` `tmp/work/cortexa8hf-vfp-neon-poky-linux-gnueabi/helloworld/0.1-r0/helloworld.c`. It will look like this:

```
#include <stdio.h>

int main(int argc, char **argv)
{
    printf("Hello World! Patched from bbappend !\n");

    return 0;
}
```

Now, based on this experimentation, let's discuss what we have done.

Contents of layers

We have already discussed, layers are a way of organizing our metadata. To use these layers, we have to follow a well-defined directory structure to keep the metadata as well as code, for the organization of this metadata. In this section, we will discuss how this organization is accomplished, what the minimum requirements of the directory structure are, and what contents are available under each directory. To talk about the directories in any layer, the layer should have at least two directories, which are discussed in the upcoming sections.

The conf directory

The minimal content in this directory is the configuration file named `layer.conf`. Basically, there are two types of layers:

- General layers
- BSP layers

We have created a general layer in the previous experimentation, using the `yocto-layer` command with its `create` option. BSP layers can be created using the `yocto-bsp` command, in a manner that is similar to using some extra options, which are not very different. This file sets all the basic properties of a layer. Our `layer.conf` file looks like this:

```
$ cat ../meta-test/conf/layer.conf
# We have a conf and classes directory, add to BBPATH
BBPATH .= ":${LAYERDIR}"

# We have recipes-* directories, add to BBFILES
BBFILES += "${LAYERDIR}/recipes-*/*/*.bb \
        ${LAYERDIR}/recipes-*/*/*.bbappend"

BBFILE_COLLECTIONS += "test"
BBFILE_PATTERN_test = "^${LAYERDIR}/"
BBFILE_PRIORITY_test = "7"
```

We may ask ourselves this question: "What we are trying to achieve with this configuration file?" We need to provide a build system, with the required information about the metadata kept in our layer, so that it can be integrated and used with other available metadata. To achieve this goal, we hook our information to the build system. How do we do this? We set information related to us, that is, our layer in commonly available configuration variables. Before proceeding further, prepare yourself to enter the environment of the helloworld recipe, using the following command. We will use this command extensively in the upcoming discussion:

```
$ bitbake -e helloworld > env-hello.txt
```

We add our layer path to the BBPATH key variable, which is a colon-separated list of paths. We can use the sed stream editor to replace colons with \ and newline characters with better visualizations. So, the grep and sed command combination turns out to be similar to the following:

```
$  grep BBPATH= env-hello.txt | sed 's/\:/\:\\\n/g'
```

This results in the following output:

```
BBPATH="/home/irfan/yocto/poky/meta-yocto:\
/home/irfan/yocto/poky/build_bbb:\
/home/irfan/yocto/poky/meta:\
/home/irfan/yocto/poky/meta-test:\
/home/irfan/yocto/poky/meta-yocto-bsp:\
/home/irfan/yocto/poky/meta-ybdevelop"
```

> Note the usage of . = and :. Only distribution layers such as meta-yocto can use the reverse of these operators to increase their precedence over other layers.

Next, we set the locations to look for *.bb and *.bbappend files in the BBFILES variable. This command indicates that you look for recipes and append files in each directory present under recipes-* directories. BBFILES is space-separated list of recipes and appended files. We can use the grep and sed combination, which is similar to the preceding code, apart from a slight modification that includes spaces instead of colons. The following is the command that is used:

```
$ grep BBFILES= env-hello.txt | sed 's/\ /\\\n/g'
```

This results in the following output:

```
BBFILES="/home/irfan/yocto/poky/meta/recipes-*/*/*.bb\
/home/irfan/yocto/poky/meta-test/recipes-*/*/*.bb\
/home/irfan/yocto/poky/meta-test/recipes-*/*/*.bbappend\
/home/irfan/yocto/poky/meta-yocto/recipes-*/*/*.bb\
/home/irfan/yocto/poky/meta-yocto/recipes-*/*/*.bbappend\
/home/irfan/yocto/poky/meta-yocto-bsp/recipes-*/*/*.bb\
/home/irfan/yocto/poky/meta-yocto-bsp/recipes-*/*/*.bbappend\
/home/irfan/yocto/poky/meta-ybdevelop/recipes-*/*/*.bb\
/home/irfan/yocto/poky/meta-ybdevelop/recipes-*/*/*.bbappend"
```

We use asterisk(*) as a wild card, in order to avoid any manual listing of the directories; then we use directory naming, which is prefixed with recipes, while creating recipes append containing recipes. This is just a convention that is followed. You can also specify any directory under your layer in order to keep your files there. Let's try not to break this convention and run into trouble.

Next, we need to add/register our name to the known and configured list of layers maintained by the build system. We do this so that when we're looking for recipes and append files, the list should look into paths we set in BBFILES. To achieve this, we add our name, test in this case, to BBFILE_COLLECTIONS. As the name suggests, this is collection of recipes. It is space-separated list of layer names. Run the grep and sed combination in a manner that's similar to the preceding one:

```
$ grep BBFILE_COLLECTIONS= env-hello.txt | sed 's/\ /\\\n/g'
```

We get the following output:

```
BBFILE_COLLECTIONS="\
core\
test\
yocto\
yoctobsp\
ybdevelop"
```

This contains our name. Now we are familiar with the build system.

The next question that remains is this: what is it that belongs to us and how should it be determined? This question is answered using BBFILE_PATTERN_<layer>, which is BBFILE_PATTERN_test in our case. So, we set this to "^${LAYERDIR}/". Again, check the environment for the value of the variable that we get:

```
$ grep BBFILE_PATTERN_test= env-hello.txt
BBFILE_PATTERN_test="^/home/irfan/yocto/poky/meta-test/"
```

So, all that starts with our provided pattern string belongs to us or our layer named test.

We have seen that our simplest build uses five layers. Real-world projects can have many more layers than this. What if we have the same recipe in multiple layers? Say, what if we have a simple recipe to confuse the build system? This needs some kind of mechanism for prioritization. We need to set the priority for our layer. This is done so that in the case of a tie, the recipe that comes from the layer with the highest priority is selected. 1 is the minimum value for the priority, and it increases with an increase in the number. So, the layer with a priority value of 7 has higher chances of its recipe being used, than the one with a priority value of 6.

 A recipe that comes from the layer with a low priority is not selected, even if it has a higher version, that is, the PV value.

What if our layer depends on some other layer? We can identify this as well using LAYERDEPEND_<layer> and provide a space-separated list of layers. Also, if we do not set a priority for our layer, these layers will be used to set the priority. If no priority calculation mechanism is successful, the default layer priority will be set to 1.

recipes-* director{y,ies}

The recipes-* directory contains recipes. For the classification of our recipes, we can have multiple recipes- directories whose type names are appended to recipes-. In the case of BSP Layers, there is usually a recipes-bsp directory to hold BSP-specific metadata. For general layers examples, we can take a look at recipes-* directories under meta-yocto.

Classes

This directory holds `classes` and `.bbclass` files, which provide logic for inheritance, so that we can place commonly used functionalities somewhere, and then reuse them across multiple recipes. It will reside inside our top-level layer directory. Here, we are talking about our layer, which is `meta-test`. Each layer can have its own classes directory and, hence, its own `.bbclass` files.

COPYING.mit

This file contains the licensing information. The script generates this for the MIT creative common license. You can modify it according to your needs, or you can choose your own. We are good with this license type, so we will keep it as it is.

README

Layers are supposed to be separate SCM entities, so it is best to keep a `README` file in them. You can decide whether or not to keep `README` for subdirectories as well, if required.

Conditional selection based on layers

We can use `BBFILE_CO LLECTIONS` to conditionally decide which recipes to include in our `BBFILES`. To do this, we need to use logic that is similar to the following in our `layer.conf`:

1. Firstly, add the following two lines to our `layer.conf` file:

```
BBFILES += "${@' '.join('${LAYERDIR}/%s/recipes-*/*/*.bbappend' %
layer \
                for layer in BBFILE_COLLECTIONS.split())}"
BBFILES += "${@' '.join('${LAYERDIR}/%s/recipes-*/*/*.bb' % layer
\
                for layer in BBFILE_COLLECTIONS.split())}"
```

2. Secondly, arrange your `recipes-*` directories under directories named according to other layers found in `BBFILE_COLLECTION`. For example, we might need to add some metadata that is specific only to it, and we want it applied only when we have `meta-ti` included in our `bblayers.conf` file. What we will do in this case is create a directory under our layer—say, `test/meta-t/`—and move all of the `recipe-*` directories specific to it under this directory. In the current configuration, this won't be applied, as there is no meta-ti layer added to our `bblayers.conf` file.

An example of such a layer is available, `meta-mel` at `https://git.yoctoproject.org/cgit/cgit.cgi/meta-mentor/tree/meta-mel/conf/layer.conf`. If you go one level up from `meta-mentor`, that is, `https://git.yoctoproject.org/cgit/cgit.cgi/`, you will find a long list of directories that already have available layers, and you can see that `meta-ti` is also there.

Append files

We did not create a recipe file while creating the meta-test layer. Instead, we created an append file for the `helloworld` recipe, which we already have in the `meta-ybdevelop` layer. Append files are a mechanism used to override/enhance existing functionality in the recipe to which the append is being applied. This is the recommended way to do things. According to the guidelines, it is suggested that you use append files instead of copying the full recipe files to your layers. These files should have `bbappend` as an extension, and the name should be the same as the recipe to which we are applying modifications. Also, you should only be modifying the contents required by you. In this append file, we used two lines. In the first line, we extended the file lookup path to be used, as follows:

```
FILESEXTRAPATHS_prepend := "${THISDIR}/${PN}-${PV}:"
```

In the next line, we picked the patch file to be applied to the source code file of our helloworld recipe. This is a simple patch file, which just changes the print message:

```
SRC_URI_append = " file://print.patch"
```

To observe the effects of this change, we did not build the full recipe. Rather, we chose a shortcut or ran it till the `do_patch` task so that we could observe the effect of our applied change. The final file that will be used by the `do_compile` task contains our applied changed, as is clear by viewing the contents of the resulting `helloworld.c` in `WORKDIR`.

This is a simple case; let's discuss a more generic use case. We are dealing with packages and image creation most of the time. We can modify existing images using `bbappends` for customization. All we need to do is create a directory under `meta-test/recipes-example-bbappend/`, say, `images-bbappend`. We can create a `bbappend` file for the image we want to customize, for example, `core-image-sato.bbappend`. We want `helloworld` to be automatically added to the image when we build `core-image-sato`. To do this, add the following to this file:

```
IMAGE_INSTALL = "helloworld"
inherit core-image
```

To quickly verify the effect, run this:

```
$ bitbake -e core-image-sato > env-sato.txt
$ grep IMAGE_INSTALL= env-sato.txt
```

We get the following output (or a similar one):

```
IMAGE_INSTALL="helloworld kernel-modules kernel-devicetree"
```

 We can also use a shortcut to customize images from our configuration file, such as `local.conf`, by adding the packages' list to `CORE_IMAGE_EXTRA_INSTALL`, as follows:
```
+= "package"
```

Packagegroups

We have discussed how to customize images using the append file on images, or using configuration files. These techniques are useful in some use cases, yet they could become a hassle in cases where we are dealing with logs of packages and we want to use these packages with more than one image type. In such cases, we will be performing duplications, which are certainly not clean. To avoid such cases, `packagegroups` comes into play. The idea is to keep these lists of packages separate from image append files so that they can be used across multiple images.

This is a specialized recipe `.bb` file with the following features. Again, it will reside in the top-level directory of our `layer/recipes-*/packagegroups/<packagegroup>.bb` file:

- It inherits package groups, that is, the `packagegroup.bbclass` class is used from meta/classes. This should be the first line of the code:

```
Inherit packagegroup
```

- All of the packagegroups that need to be created are added to the `PACKAGES` variable:

```
PACKAGES = "PG1 PG2"
```

- Packages required for runtime are added to the `RDEPENDS_<pacagroupname>` conditional override:

```
RDEPENDS_PG1 = "P1 P2 ... PN"
RDEPENDS_PG2 = "P1 P2 ... PN"
```

- Similarly, we can add `RRECOMMENDS_<packagroupname>` conditional override to `RRECOMMENDS` packages:

```
RRECOMMENDS_PG1 = "P1 P2 … PN"
RRECOMMENDS_PG2 = "P1 P2 … PN"
```

- To build with either of these `packagegroups`, we need to add the `packagegroup` to `IMAGE_INSTALL` in the image's `bbappend` file. Thus, we can use this list across multiple packages.

If you are still confused regarding this concept, don't worry at all. We will practically arrange all our metadata using these concepts.

Summary

In this chapter, we created one more `meta-test` layer. We also performed some experimentation on this layer so that we could discuss related concepts. We discussed the contents of layers in detail, and we also discussed image customization techniques using simple configuration, `bbappend`, and `packagegroups`.

In next chapter, we will discuss some console-based games. For this purpose, we will select a console-based version of the popular game PAC-MAN.

6
Your First Console Game

In the previous chapter, we talked about layers. So far, we have formulated the basis of Yocto Project. Now, we need to move toward practical development. Going forward with this goal in mind, we will add a console-based game to our board. For this purpose, we have selected PAC-MAN. We will create a recipe for this game and enable it so that it can be added to our `rootfs`.

Hardware requirements

The following is a list of the hardware required to run this game:

- BeagleBone Black
- HDMI display (in my case, a Samsung LED TV)
- An HDMI cable for the display connection
- A USB keyboard

For testing purposes, we can use the following simple hardware:

- BeagleBone Black
- SSH using USB or an Ethernet cable.

Pacman4Console

PAC-MAN is a popular computer game of legacy times. It is hard to consider someone not knowing or not even having played it. We can find the code for GUI-based versions, but our major concern is not the game; we want to learn to code it using something practical. We will be using PAC-MAN for console by *Mike Billars* from `https://sites.google.com/site/doctormike/pacman.html`. We are choosing this for its simplicity. From this location, we got the link to the source Git as well as the source tar balls. We will use the Git link.

Let's develop our recipe

We need to collect different pieces for our recipe. As our prime purpose is learning, we won't list a final working recipe for our package. Rather, we will keep on experimenting and modifying our recipe and explain what we have been doing wrong or what we have been missing in the previous version or step. We already have a recipe in our `meta-ybdevelop` layer named `helloworld`. We can copy the basic elements from it and start modifying it to make our task easy.

[Copying from the existing recipe is not only required for ease, but also to avoid unnecessary mistakes.]

Basic elements

The following are the basic elements that are very easy to set, and they are shown as follows in the `helloworld` recipe:

```
DESCRIPTION = "Simple helloworld application"
SECTION = "examples"
LICENSE = "MIT"
LIC_FILES_CHKSUM = "file://${
COMMON_LICENSE_DIR}/MIT;md5=0835ade698e0bcf8506ecda2f7b4f302"
```

This will be changed to the following in the case of PAC-MAN:

```
DESCRIPTION = "Pacman for console is a console based PacMan"
SECTION = "games"
LICENSE = "GPLv2"
LIC_FILES_CHKSUM = "file://${
WORKDIR}/git/COPYING;md5=751419260aa954499f7abaabaa882bbe"
```

Let's discuss these elements:

- `DESCRIPTION`: Put whatever you like, but put something that can be understood

- `SECTION`: Let's say this is about games

- `LICENSE`: The author of the game has chosen `GPLv2`, and so have we

- `LIC_FILES_CHKSUM`: We have a license file named `COPYING` in the Git repository, and this will be fetched to `WORKDIR`, so we set the license to a certain point in this file, and MD5 is calculated using the `md5sum` command

Source control

The next task is related to source fetching. We need to set the `SRC_URI` variable to a successful value so that our source code is successfully fetched. From the preceding link, we can get the link to a Git repository, which is located at `https://gitorious.org`. As gitorious is shutting down its services, I have placed the repository with due permissions from its creator at `https://github.com/YoctoForBeaglebone/`. Using this information, let's set this to the following:

```
SRC_URI = "git://gitorious.org/
patches-and-mirrors/pacman4console.git;branch=master"
```

For GitHub, this is the code:

```
SRC_URI = "git://github.com/YoctoForBeaglebone/
pacman4console.git;branch=master"
```

Having specified the source repository, let's give it a try by executing the following build command:

```
$ bitbake pacman4console
```

After issuing the preceding command, we get errors that are similar to the following:

```
ERROR: Function failed: Fetcher failure for URL: 'git://gitorious.org/
patches-and-mirrors/pacman4console.git;branch=master'. Please set a valid
SRCREV for url ['SRCREV_default_pn-pacman4console', 'SRCREV_default',
'SRCREV_pn-pacman4console', 'SRCREV'] (possible key names are git://
gitorious.org/patches-and-mirrors/pacman4console.git;branch=master, or
use a ;rev=X URL parameter)
```

There are two possible solutions that can correct this, and both are pointed out in the error message itself:

- The first solution is to set the `SRCREV` variable to a valid hash, or if we want to check for the latest on each build, then we can set it to `${AUTOREV}`. Using this approach, our successful source fetching code will become this:

  ```
  SRCREV = "${AUTOREV}"
  SRC_URI = "git://gitorious.org/patches-and-
  mirrors/pacman4console.git;branch=master"
  ```

- The second solution, which is also pointed out in the error message, is to use some `rev` using the `rev=X` syntax, where `;` is the option separator and `X` is a valid revision. Using this approach, our successful source fetching code will be this:

  ```
  SRC_URI = "git://gitorious.org/patches-and-mirrors/
  pacman4console.git;rev=master"
  ```

Work directory and version

Let's save our recipe as `pacman4console_git.bb`. Build it by running BitBake
or generate an environment with the `-e` option and look for `${WORKDIR}` in the
environment or physically in the filesystem. Using the environment, we get the
following result:

```
$ bitbake pacman4console -e | grep ^WORKDIR

WORKDIR="/home/irfan/yocto/poky/build_bbb/tmp/work/
cortexa8hf-vfp-neon-poky-linux-gnueabi/pacman4console/git-r0"
```

If you remember what we learned in *Chapter 3, Creating the helloworld Recipe*, `WORKDIR`
is named `${PV}-${PR}`, which turns to `git-r0` here. We have not specified the `PR`
value, so it is set to the default, which is `r0`. This kind of work directory name is
fine if there is no active development on the repository, but it won't be very helpful
otherwise. We will want our `WORKDIR` variable to contain revisions in cases such as
`SVN` or hash tags for Git, which is done by adding the following line to our recipe
after changing the `PV` value:

```
PV  = "1.2-git${SRCPV}"
```

Let's rerun the preceding command to get a new value for `WORKDIR` from the
environment:

```
$  bitbake pacman4console -e | grep ^WORKDIR

WORKDIR="/home/irfan/yocto/poky/build_bbb/tmp/work/cortexa8hf-vfp-neon-
poky-linux-gnueabi/pacman4console/1.2-gitAUTOINC+ddc229c347-r0"
```

This contains the Git hash appended by the + sign. For each new build, if there is any
change in the remote repository, our work directory will be appended with the latest
commit hash to reflect this, thus helping us debug situations.

The S directory

Usually, this is the same as `WORKDIR`, but that's not always the case. In the case of
Git, we have the Git directory under it. We need to tell BitBake where it can find the
sources, and we can do this using the following line:

```
S = "${WORKDIR}/git"
```

Should this be it? Is our recipe ready? Looks like it. Let's verify whether this is the
case or not by building it and analyzing the contents. To do this, run the following
command:

```
$  bitbake -c cleansstate pacman4console; bitbake pacman4console
```

Finally, the last line of the output is:

```
…..................................      Skipping the rest        ........
..................................
NOTE: Tasks Summary: Attempted 372 tasks of which 360 didn't need to be
rerun and all succeeded.
```

After taking a look at this output, we are very hopeful; everything that remains is taken care of by BitBake itself. This can be the case for most of the packages that have a Makefile or build setup based upon `autotools` available. So, our next step will be to take a look at the contents of the `deploy-ipks` subdirectory of `WORKDIR`. Run a tree command on it:

```
$  tree deploy-ipks/
```

You'll get the following output:

```
deploy-ipks/
└── cortexa8hf-vfp-neon
    ├── pacman4console-dbg_1.2-git0+ddc229c347-r0_cortexa8hf-vfp-neon.ipk
    └── pacman4console-dev_1.2-git0+ddc229c347-r0_cortexa8hf-vfp-neon.ipk
1 directory, 2 files
```

This is not what is desired, and we have only `dbg` and `dev` packages. If we open these packages with the archive manager, we can see that they are empty. Also, if we take a look at other directories, most of them are empty or contain nothing useful. So, we need to do more.

Debugging compile tasks

To see what is actually happening, let's launch `devshell` using the following command:

```
$ bitbake -c devshell pacman4console
```

In the launched `devshell`, let's run Make, which is expected to run in our case, and see the results. We get the following output. We'll skip redundant warnings to avoid an unnecessary rush in the output:

```
gcc pacman.c      -o pacman        -DDATAROOTDIR=\"/usr/local/share\
"    -O2 -pipe -g -feliminate-unused-debug-types -Wl,-O1 -Wl,
--hash-style=gnu -Wl,--as-needed -lncurses
pacman.c: In function 'LoadLevel':
```

```
pacman.c:393:10: warning: ignoring return value of 'fscanf',
declared with attribute warn_unused_result [-Wunused-result]
    fscanf(fin, "%d", &Level[a][b]);
         ^

gcc pacmanedit.c -o pacmanedit -DDATAROOTDIR=\"/usr/local/share\
"  -O2 -pipe -g -feliminate-unused-debug-types -Wl,-O1 -Wl,--
hash-style=gnu -Wl,--as-needed -lncurses
pacmanedit.c: In function 'LoadLevel':
```

Apart from a warning, the bigger thing to notice is gcc. How can we use
native gcc for cross-compilation? Let's take a look at the Makefile itself.
Here, we have gcc hardcoded:

```
all:
   gcc pacman.c       -o pacman      -DDATAROOTDIR=\"$(datarootdir)\"
$(CPPFLAGS) $(CFLAGS) $(LDFLAGS) -lncurses
```

We cannot use it this way; the compiler should be set from the environment, so
let's modify our Makefile. For future usage, we will create a patch for this purpose.
Our sources come from Git. We can go to unpacked sources placed under the Git
directory, make desired modifications, and issue the git diff command and save
the output to a file. The contents of our patch will look similar to the following:

```
diff --git a/Makefile b/Makefile
index c261974..1e4b2a2 100644
--- a/Makefile
+++ b/Makefile
@@ -2,9 +2,11 @@ prefix=/usr/local
 bindir=$(prefix)/bin
 datarootdir=$(prefix)/share

+CC?=gcc
+
 all:
-        gcc pacman.c       -o pacman      -DDATAROOTDIR=\
"$(datarootdir)\" $(CPPFLAGS) $(CFLAGS) $(LDFLAGS) -lncurses
-        gcc pacmanedit.c -o pacmanedit -DDATAROOTDIR=\
"$(datarootdir)\" $(CPPFLAGS) $(CFLAGS) $(LDFLAGS) -lncurses
+        $(CC) pacman.c       -o pacman      -DDATAROOTDIR=\
"$(datarootdir)\" $(CPPFLAGS) $(CFLAGS) $(LDFLAGS) -lncurses
+        $(CC) pacmanedit.c -o pacmanedit -DDATAROOTDIR=\
"$(datarootdir)\" $(CPPFLAGS) $(CFLAGS) $(LDFLAGS) -lncurses

 install:       all
        mkdir -p $(DESTDIR)$(bindir)
```

We will place this in the files directory under the `pacman4console` directory, which contains our recipe. Also, we will modify `SRC_URI` to add this, which will be changed to the following:

```
SRC_URI = "git://gitorious.org/patches-and-mirrors/pacman4console.
git;branch=master \
        file://makefile.patch"
```

After making these changes to the recipe and saving the run build until the compilation step, verify the generation of required contents in the work directory. `WORDIR` should have two binaries generated in it, namely `pacman` and `pacmanedit`.

Installing a task

Apparently, Makefile has an installation target available, so we should be able to use this target in our recipe as well. To do this, let's add a `do_install` task in the recipe, as follows:

```
do_install () {
  oe_runmake install
}
```

Now, let's try to run the same recipe to install the task using the following command line:

```
$  bitbake -c cleansstate pacman4console; bitbake -c install
pacman4console
```

This will also end with an error like this:

```
| mkdir -p /usr/bin
| cp pacman /usr/bin
| cp: cannot create regular file '/usr/bin/pacman': Permission denied
```

Again, the problem seems similar to that of native path usage. Take a look at Makefile, and you should notice that `DESTDIR` is the variable that needs to be provided with the value where we want our contents to be installed. We have a special variable `D`, which points to a destination directory, which actually points to an image directory under `WORKDIR`. So, our problem should be resolved if we set `DESTDIR` to `${D}`, as follows:

```
do_install () {
  oe_runmake DESTDIR="${D}" install
}
```

Run the preceding command again, without errors, to verify the success. Also, take a look at the contents of WORKDIR to validate the creation of the image directory. You can verify that all of the contents that we are copying in the installation target of Maker are now present under this directory in the respective directory structure.

Adding package contents

Running the preceding command combination again with the build task omits -c install in the second part of the command after we get the following error message. This message is related to packaging:

```
ERROR: QA Issue: pacman4console: Files/directories were installed but
not shipped
  /usr/share
  /usr/share/pacman
  /usr/share/pacman/Levels
....................................................
  /usr/share/pacman/Levels/level06.dat
ERROR: QA run found fatal errors. Please consider fixing them.
ERROR: Function failed: do_package_qa
```

Clearly, the first line of Error: explains the cause of this error. To fix this, we need to add these files to the package we want these files to be part of. We choose this to be the default package using the following command line in our recipe:

```
FILES_${PN} += " \
  /usr/share/ \
  /usr/share/pacman \
  /usr/share/pacman/Levels \
  /usr/share/pacman/Levels/level05.dat \
  /usr/share/pacman/Levels/level04.dat \
  /usr/share/pacman/Levels/template.dat \
  /usr/share/pacman/Levels/level07.dat \
  /usr/share/pacman/Levels/level02.dat \
  /usr/share/pacman/Levels/README \
  /usr/share/pacman/Levels/level08.dat \
  /usr/share/pacman/Levels/level09.dat \
  /usr/share/pacman/Levels/level01.dat \
  /usr/share/pacman/Levels/level03.dat \
  /usr/share/pacman/Levels/level06.dat \
  "
```

Save the recipe, build again using the same command as the preceding one, and analyze the contents of WORKDIR. Validate all of the contents as expected; we can find our generic package in deploy-dir. Also, you can check the contents of the package using the archive manager. It contains both binaries, pacman and pacmanedit, in usr/bin and the data for the supporting levels in usr/share. We can transfer this ipk to our board using any of the available options. Copy it to the card and install it using opkg install pacman4console_1.2-git0+ddc229c347-r0_cortexa8hf-vfp-neon.ipk or by transferring via SSH and using the same command to install it.

Adding a package to the root filesystem

To add this package to our root filesystem, we will use the following approach, and we will follow the same approach for subsequent packages throughout the book:

- Create a packagegroup named packagegroup-yb-develop under meta-ybdevelop/recipes-example/
- Add an appended image to include the preceding packagegroup instance

packagegroup

We will name this packagegroup-yb-develop.bb. It will be created under a subdirectory named packagegroups, and it will contain the following content by the end of this chapter:

```
SUMMARY = "Packagegroup For our layer YB-Develop"
LICENSE = "MIT"
PR = "r1"
inherit packagegroup
RDEPENDS_${PN} = "pacman4console \
        helloworld\
    "
```

We will use this packagegroup instance for any further package addition throughout the book.

Image bbappend

We will add this file to the images subdirectory under our `meta-ybdevelop/` `recipes-example/` directory. It will be named `images/core-image-sato.` `bbappend`. This will contain only this single line for now. We may not need to add anything else to it in the future:

```
IMAGE_INSTALL_append = " packagegroup-yb-develop"
```

Action

All is set now; just run the following command and wait for the completion:

```
$ bitbake core-image-sato
```

By the time this command is complete, the resulting image created by it will have `pacman4console` added to it. Just burn it to the SD card using scripts and enjoy.

Summary

In this chapter, we created a recipe for the popular game PAC-MAN's console-based version. We went through the development of different tasks gradually, discussing successful as well as failed steps and explaining them.

In the next chapter, we will learn how to use BeagleBone for a simple surveillance system.

7
Turning BeagleBone into a Home Surveillance System

In the previous chapter, you learned how to create a console-based application. We went through the evolutionary phase of development for learning purposes. In this chapter, we will explore different options to turn our BeagleBone Black board into a home surveillance system. On this path, we will encounter some hurdles and come up with solutions to those. In a fully prepared system, the actual execution block may not consist of more than one line of a GStreamer pipeline. However, it will be a long journey to get to this. We know the significance of layers from the previous chapter. In this chapter, we will use some of the community or vendor maintained layers, such as `meta-oe` and `meta-ti`.

Problem statement

Let's assume we want to view some place in our home, say garage, from another part of our home or office. However, we don't want to spend a lot to fulfill this *wish*. We just want to use existing stuff available to us. Fortunately, we have the following two components available:

- BeagleBone Black
- Webcam C110 (Logitech)

Furthermore, we want to use generic webcams, not specialized ones.

Requirements

The next logical step is to break the problem statement into pieces so that we can attack them one by one, or we may luckily find some solution that solves all parts of the problem. Hardware requirements are already mentioned. So, here is the breakdown:

- Capture video data from the web camera
- Encode video data
- Push packed video data to network
- Receive video data from network
- Play the received video data

Software fulfilling these types of requirements are called **multimedia frameworks**. In the OSS world, they have such frameworks. The most popular of these is GStreamer. We used it in *Chapter 4, Adding Multimedia to Your Board*.

Existing solutions / literature survey

We are a millennial generation. We love to use technology and if we are from a technical background then why not? So, the search engine results for Video Streaming Using Beaglebone Black consist of the following types.

Requiring specialized capturing hardware

There are solutions that require specialized video-capturing hardware to get an encoded stream. These solutions are very good, in the sense that we don't have to perform encoding on BeagleBone. Instead, we can just use the same encoded video. All we need to do is to add N/W-related information to the data and put it on the N/W. However, this cannot be categorized as a general approach due to hardware binding. Users need to have a specialized camera, which I don't like.

Requiring specialized software application

Some of the solutions have created their own applications for most of the tasks, especially to capture video data from a camera. For specialized tasks, these solutions are certainly good options where you know things won't change. However, for learning purposes, such solutions seem to have some limitations. For learning, we should have a lot of options available, if not endless. Furthermore, these applications are mostly created using existing frameworks, but for each small change, you will need a recompilation or packaging of applications.

Based on Debian/Angstrom

BeagleBone Black has images available for Debian- and Angstrom-based distributions. So, there are solutions that refer to these distributions. In the case of Debian, you have the ease of fetching prebuilt binaries directly to the boards. It is easy for users who have no development experience, but not recommended for developers. Angstrom-based solutions are closer to the one we are looking for.

Selected solution

Since I already mentioned in the requirements that we have a popular multimedia framework available called GStreamer, we will go for it. This is not rocket science. We will enable it in our `rootfs`. Certainly, we will face issues. However, we will hit our heads against these issues and resolve them. The answer to our problems is in the form of plugins. This way, we will enable BeagleBone to capture the stream from the attached webcam and serve it over our network to the client side.

Host/server side (BeagleBone)

A webcam will be attached to BeagleBone, and it will stream what is captured. The following are some of the requirements:

- `v4l2src`: This is a plugin for reading from Video4Linux2-based devices, which is the Video I/O API and driver framework. Using this, we will widen the choice of our capture devices. These plugins run in user space. They call kernel IOCTL to communicate with the underlying kernel space driver for particular sensors plugged in via the USB of BeagleBone.

- Video decoder: We have a lot of video decoder options available to us. We can choose from the available ones, or we can build some extra codecs, which are not built by default, such as x264, VP8, and so on. We can choose different resolutions, bitrates, and other options to optimize output according to our requirements.

- `rtp{codec}pay`: This adds RTP information to data.

- `udpsin`: This is the sink element for sending packets over UDP.

Client side

Physically, client side is a desktop or laptop machine, where we will view the output of our webcam. The webcam is attached to BeagleBone and available on the network. On client side, we have multiple options, two of which are listed here:

- VLC: This is a popular video player
- GStreamer: We can use the reverse pipeline for GStreamer

Let's start the fun

Having discussed the strategy / action plan, we are ready to start the implementation. We have the tools ready with us. We can start using them. We have the Yocto Project directory structure available. Currently, we have the following layers added to our `bblayers.conf` file, which is present in our build directory under the `conf` subdirectory:

```
BBLAYERS ?= " \
        /home/irfan/yocto/poky/meta \
        /home/irfan/yocto/poky/meta-yocto \
        /home/irfan/yocto/poky/meta-yocto-bsp \
        /home/irfan/yocto/poky/meta-ybdevelop \
    "
```

First, let's check whether we have GStreamer recipes provided by the existing layers. You can use `find` inside the Yocto Project directory to investigate this as follows:

```
$ find ./meta* -name gst*
```

The results show that we have GStreamer recipes available in `meta/recipes-multimedia/`.

If we have a look at this directory, we could find many recipes. At a higher level, these recipes can be broken into two type of recipes based on the GStreamer version. There are two major versions, 0.10 and 1.0, of GStreamer available. We will use the 0.10 version. Other than these two versions, we have four types of recipes as described in the following sections. `gstreamer_0.10.36.bb` is the core GStreamer library recipe, and the other four are related to the four plugin types of GStreamer.

Base plugins

These are a basic set of plugins that have enough support from the community.

Good plugins

These are plugins that are supported by the community and have no licensing issues.

Bad plugins

These plugins are not well tested.

Ugly plugins

These plugins are supported well, but most of them are reverse-engineered ones. So, you should be very careful if you are distributing these plugins.

There are a few more recipes that do not fall into these general categories. These are extra codecs that can be added if required. For example, FFmpeg consists of a full set of audio video codecs and format wrappers.

Enabling GStreamer and plugins

We will use `packagegroup-yb-develope`, as we have used in the previous chapters, to enable GStreamer and all the plugins. We can pick and choose from the required plugins. All of them can be enabled by adding the following line to the `packagegroup-yb-develope.bb` file under `meta-yb-develope/recipes-examples` to the variable `RDEPENDS_${PN}`:

```
gstreamer \
gst-plugins-base \
gst-plugins-good-meta \
gst-plugins-good \
gst-plugins-bad \
gst-plugins-ugly \
```

 You will have to use white listing for ugly plugins in your `local.conf` or `auto.conf` file as we did in *Chapter 4, Adding Multimedia to Your Board*, as follows:
```
LICENSE_FLAGS_WHITELIST = "commercial"
```

Choosing which of these plugins needs to be built depends on the choice of codecs we want to use in our application/pipeline. We may not need an ugly set of plugins. Alternatively, we should not be shipping these with our products. Instead, we can provide usage instructions to the user.

This package group is already added to `core-image-sato`. We can just build it using the following command line to have our root filesystem. Let's try it:

```
$ bitbake core-image-sato
```

The image that is created is GStreamer enabled. We can verify this by extracting the `rootfs` image created and looking for GST-related stuff in the `image/usr/lib/gstreamer` and `gstreamer-0.1` directories. This is a hacky way. We can also flash this image and run the following command on the board:

```
$ gst-inspect
```

This is a GStreamer tool, along with many other useful tools such as `gst-launch`, that we will use. This tool would show us all the available plugins for different codecs, source elements, or sink elements if it is provided without any argument. It would give us detailed information about an element if we give that element as input to this tool. For example, we want to know what different capabilities and arguments a particular element supports. For `autovideosrc`, we will use the following command:

```
$ gst-inspect udpsrc
```

This will list detailed information about the `udpsrc` element. Some of the sections that this tool shows are as follows:

- **Factory Details**: This includes details such as long name, class, description, and author(s) of the element
- **Plugin Details**: This shows the name, description, library filename with full path, version, and license of the element
- **Element Flags**: This shows the flags for the element
- **Element Properties**: This shows the properties of the element, such as name, format, buffers, device if required, flags, and so on

Enabling Video4Linux2

When we build the preceding configuration, deploy our images, and load our board with these images, we should find out whether:

- We have GStreamer available
- We have the GStreamer tools gst-inspect and gst-launch available
- We have an element available to fulfill our requirements

With the images that we built, we can verify the availability of GStreamer and its tools, but we fail to verify that we have an element to fulfill our requirements. Why is that? We don't have an element `v4l2src`, which is required to capture images. We can move further from here. Further investigation is required to know why we don't have it. As we can see from the `http://gstreamer.freedesktop.org/data/doc/gstreamer/head/gst-plugins-good-plugins/html/` link, the package group we added earlier contains the `v4l2src` element. We need to further investigate by looking at the recipe of `gst-plugins-good0.10.31.bb`. We get the following line in this recipe:

```
PACKAGECONFIG[v4l] = "--with-libv4l2,--without-libv4l2,libv4l"
```

This line shows that we can optionally enable or disable `v4l`. We have three options to enable it.

In-place amendment

Edit the `gst-plugins-good0.10.31.bb` file directly and add the following line to it:

```
PACKAGECONFIG += "v4l"
```

This line builds the package with the `-libv4l2` option. Although this method will work, it is not recommended as it is not a clean approach.

Using append

We can create an append file for the main `gst-plugins-good0.10.31.bb` recipe in `meta-yb-develope/recipes-multipmedia/gstreamer/` as `gst-plugins-good0.10.31.bbappend` and add the following line to it:

```
PACKAGECONFIG = "v4l"
```

This is the most appropriate and recommended way.

Using local.conf

If you are a lazy person like me and the second approach seems an overkill for you, then you could use another syntax in your `local.conf` or `auto.conf` file to achieve the preceding effect:

```
PACKAGECONFIG_append_pn-gst-plugins-good = "v4l"
```

Remember that this is a combination of append and pn to make it conditional and easy.

> If you want to use x264 encoder, you would need to add the following line as well to `local.conf` or `auto.conf`:
>
> **PACKAGECONFIG_append_pn-gst-plugins-ugly = "x264"**
>
> Alternatively, you can use other approaches to enable it. Otherwise, use other codecs.

To build the package with either of these approaches, we should have v4l2src in our root filesystem. However, life is not that simple, at least for the works where R&D is involved. The problem is that there is dependency on the v4l-utils package, which is not available. So, we will get an error while building this package. To resolve this problem, we need to provide the v4l-utils package. This package is not available in Poky, yet it is available in meta-oe/meta-oe. Let's clone it using the following command in the Yocto Project directory, which contains Poky itself:

```
$ git clone -b daisy git@github.com:openembedded/meta-oe.git
```

This will create a meta-oe directory, which itself contains another meta-oe subdirectory. To enable this layer, we need to add its path to bblayers.conf as follows:

```
/home/irfan/yocto/meta-oe/meta-oe \
```

Now, our bblayers.conf file is changed. Running the bitbake command again will be successful.

The next step is to construct the GStreamer pipeline.

The GStreamer pipeline

This is the GStreamer pipeline. We will use this pipeline after we prepare the hardware setup:

```
# gst-launch v4l2src device=/dev/video0 ! 'video/x-raw-
yuv,width=320,height=240' ! x264enc pass=qual quantizer=20
tune=zerolatency ! rtph264pay ! udpsink host=192.168.1.5 port=5000
```

You should know the maximum support provided by the sensor you bought, as `gst-lauch` requests the parameters given here to the driver of your camera. If your camera supports 720p (HD) but not 1080p (full HD), then requesting a width of 1920 and height of 1080 is useless. It will simply throw an error, or in some cases it may not even do that, depending on the implementation of the underlying driver. You should also know the frames per second supported by your camera to increase the streaming quality.

The `gst-lauch` tool provided by GStreamer is used to run a pipeline of elements. All the elements are separated by an exclamation symbol (`!`), as shown in the preceding pipeline.

 Verbosity can be set using the `-v` option. Verbosity level can be increased appending many V alphabets, such as `-vv`, `-vvv`, and so on. Thus, we will know the input and output properties, caps, used by default.

Let's go through the elements one by one:

- `V4l2src`: This video captures the source plugin.
- `video/x-raw-yuv,width=320,height=240`: Here, we are setting the input video type and resolutions.
- `x264enc`: This is a h264 video encoder. I chose it for its popularity of good results on lower bit rates. You can use other (Theora, VP8, and so on) video codecs as well if you don't want to use h264, since it comes from the ugly set of plugins.
- `Rtph264pay`: This is the RTP pay plugin.
- `Udpsink`: This is the UDP sink element. You need to specify the host where you want to receive data. You could also use multicast for this purpose if you have more than one client to serve.

 The USB video class driver should be loaded with `nodrop=1`.

Client side

In the server side, which is BeagleBone, we ran a GStreamer pipeline. This pipeline captures data from the webcam, encodes it, applies RTP headers to it, and transfers it to the system. We provided IP in the option host of `udpsink`. Now, on the client side, we need to play this video. For this, we have two options.

VLC

VLC is a popular video player. We can't imagine someone, who knows how to work with computers, not knowing the player. To use this player, we need to create a `.sdp` file, say `test.sdp`, with the following contents in it:

```
test.sdp:
v=0
m=video 5000 RTP/AVP 96
c=IN IP4 192.168.1.5
a=rtpmap:96 H264/90000
```

Open this file using the VLC player. You should be able to get the output of the webcam. We ran our server-side pipeline in the previous section. This pipeline sends the UDP packets on the machine with IP 192.168.1.5, as we specified in the pipeline using the option host at port 5000. VLC will render this video using information from this SDP file where we give the port, IP, and other video settings.

GStreamer

Another option is to use the GStreamer pipeline as follows:

```
$ gst-launch udpsrc port=5000 ! rtph264depay ! x264dec ! autovideosink
```

We don't need to specify the IP to the `udpsrc` element because it is specified in `udpsink`, which is in the pipeline running on BeagleBone. Next, two pipeline elements can have multiple combinations of the selected `encoder/decoder` and `pay/depay` elements. We have used only h264 and RTP. You should try other options as well. There is no change in the `autovideosink` unless you are using some special hardware and some custom element developed for video display.

Get ready for running and surprises

As we have already mentioned, R&D work is always full of surprises, and so is our case. Now, we will go through the surprises I faced while creating this demo, and the solutions I used.

Camera-detection issues

On my first set of images, the camera that I had with me was not being detected. On debugging a bit, I realized we are using the Yocto Project default kernel recipe, `linux-yocto`. It does not enable kernel configurations required for multimedia applications to work. So, on connecting a camera to the board, only the following output was seen:

```
usb 2-1: new high-speed USB device number 2 using musb-hdrc
```

On debugging further, I came to know that V4l2 uses the **UVC** (**USB Video Class**) driver, which was missing in my build. I had to enable the following configurations. You can verify which configurations you already have enabled by running `menuconfig`. Alternatively, you can look for them in the `.config` file, which can be found at `tmp/work/beaglebone-poky-linux-gnueabi/{linux-selected-recipe}/{KVERSION}-r22d+gitrAUTOINC+{GITHASH}/git/.config`:

```
CONFIG_MEDIA_CONTROLLER=m
CONFIG_VIDEO_DEV=m
CONFIG_VIDEO_V4L2_SUBDEV_API=y
CONFIG_VIDEO_V4L2=m
CONFIG_V4L2_MEM2MEM_DEV=m
CONFIG_VIDEOBUF_GEN=m
CONFIG_VIDEOBUF_DMA_CONTIG=m
CONFIG_VIDEOBUF2_CORE=m
CONFIG_VIDEOBUF2_MEMOPS=m
CONFIG_VIDEOBUF2_DMA_CONTIG=m
CONFIG_VIDEOBUF2_VMALLOC=m
CONFIG_USB_VIDEO_CLASS=m
CONFIG_USB_VIDEO_CLASS_INPUT_EVDEV=y
CONFIG_USB_GSPCA=m
CONFIG_V4L_PLATFORM_DRIVERS=y
CONFIG_V4L_MEM2MEM_DRIVERS=y
CONFIG_VIDEO_MEM2MEM_DEINTERLACE=m
```

Having enabled these configurations, the webcam was successfully detected. To enable these or any other required configurations, you have multiple options, which we will discuss in more detail in the next chapter. These are the options:

- You can run the `menuconfig` task using the following command:

  ```
  $ bitbake -c menuconfig virtual/kernel
  ```

  Then you can enable these configurations from the GUI.

- Simply copy these configurations to the `.config` file
- Use configuration fragments. Here's how you do it:

  1. Create the `bbappend` file for your kernel in `layer/recipes-kernel/linux/kernel-name_version.bbappend`.
  2. Add all the configurations to the `<name>.cfg` file, say `test.cfg`, and place it in `layer/recipes-kernel/linux/files/`.
  3. Add the following lines to the `bbappend` file:

     ```
     FILESEXTRAPATHS_prepend := "${THISDIR}/files:"
     SRC_URI_append = " test.cfg"
     ```

We are adding these here for reference purposes. Using kernel from *TI*, these will be enabled by default. Just be patient!

Here is the output containing the vendor info and model details:

```
usb 2-1: New USB device found, idVendor=046d, idProduct=0829
usb 2-1: New USB device strings: Mfr=1, Product=2, SerialNumber=0
usb 2-1: Product: Webcam C110
uvcvideo: Found UVC 1.00 device Webcam C110 (046d:0829)
```

UVC driver DMA issue

With the Yocto Project kernel, I had to face issues related to DMA. It was not working with DMA. It was showing something similar to the following lines, but there was no output:

```
Setting pipeline to PAUSED ...
Pipeline is live and does not need PREROLL ...
Setting pipeline to PLAYING ...
New clock: GstSystemClock
```

To solve these issues, I had to build `rootfs` with `meta-ti` so that we can use the Linux kernel provided by *TI*, which has related fixes.

Build with the meta-ti layer

Rather than trying to find fixes for different issues related to hardware, it is always wise to go for vendor-provided bits and check them first. If things are working there, we could compare or even directly use them. To achieve this, I followed these steps.

Fetch the layer

Texas Instruments' meta-ti layer is available at git.yoctoproject.org/cgit/cgit.cgi/meta-ti/. We can fetch this from the Yocto Project directory as follows:

```
$ git clone  -b daisy git://git.yoctoproject.org/meta-ti
```

Set the layer priority

Set layer priority higher than meta-yocto and meta-yocto-bsp so that duplicate content from both layers doesn't get picked and is overridden by meta-ti. For this, we have to set it in meta-ti/conf/layer.conf:

```
BBFILE_PRIORITY_meta-ti = "7"
```

 A simple solution can be the removal of meta-yocto-bsp from bblayers.conf.

Enable the layer

To enable our layer, we added the following line to our bblayers.conf file:

```
/home/irfan/yocto/meta-ti \
```

 Instead of using absolute paths like this, we can also use the $TOPDIR variable, which points to our build directory, as follows:
```
$TOPDIR/../../meta-ti \
```

We are ready to run the following image-creation command:

```
$ bitbake core-image-sato.
```

Thus, the image created will have everything functional. Happy experimenting!

Further enhancements

Having this working example in hand, we can now tweak it further for better results. To achieve this, we can experiment and explore the following areas:

- To modify `/etc/modprobe.d/modprobe.conf` to edit the `uvcvideo` module update, we should create a recipe.

- To run this pipeline on board boot up, we can create a `systemd` service so that we don't have to manually run it. We should create the service in `meta-yb-develop` using a recipe.

- We may use a vendor-provided decoder that was implemented on the DSP part of the board and leveraged full strength of the hardware. To achieve this, we can use `gstreamer-ti` from `meta-ti`. Consider this an exercise and play with it.

- Using a combination of RTSP and web server on board using lighttpd or on a local network, we can enhance user experience. Project, on the client side, you don't have to run the GStreamer pipeline or VLC manually. You just go to a web address and view the output. There can be different approaches to achieve this. Whatever technique you choose, you will need a web server to host the web page to display our video. To use the VLC plugin in a web browser, you can get instructions from `http://www.tldp.org/REF/VLC-User-Guide/x1574.html`. For this web server, we have the following two options:

  - The easiest way is to set up the web server part on our client machine where we are playing the VLC player to serve the web page that will play our video stream received at RTP. We will have to set up the web server and create a web page to embed the video in it.

  - A little bit more work would be required if we don't want an extra server and use BeagleBone as the web server. However, no matter what our choices are, we will need to add a web server package of our choice as well as use the Yocto Project, apart from setting it up and creating a web page. Also, we will use BeagleBone IP in the `host` option of our pipeline.

Summary

In this chapter, we enabled GStreamer on our board. To do this, we used extra layers tweaked with configurations. We faced issues related to debugging and resolved them. In the next chapter, we will enable our BeagleBone Black to become a Wi-Fi hotspot.

8
BeagleBone as a Wi-Fi Access Point

In the previous chapter, we created a simple solution for a home-based surveillance system. In this chapter, we will convert our BeagleBone Black into a Wi-Fi hotspot. While doing this, you will learn how to enable the required configurations in kernel and how to change different kernels. You will also learn how to change the default upstart program. Moreover, we will create a recipe to modify the filesystem so that all our configuration files are in place when we boot up the target. These configuration files are related to different components.

Problem statement / use case

Our router has stopped working as a Wi-Fi access point for some unknown reasons. Its LAN connections are working fine. Should we go to the market and buy a new router, or do I have some other options available to fix this piece at home or replace it with some other solution? I have the following hardware available:

- BeagleBone Black
- ZyXEL Wi-Fi dongle

I have been using this dongle with my old laptop, which is spare. So, can we make use of the same dongle? Can we use Yocto Project and enable our BeagleBone Black to be used along with this Wi-Fi dongle and get something working, which can solve our problem?

Requirements

We want to use these available hardware resources to solve the problem. For this, we need to have following software pieces in Yocto Project, and we will use Linux kernel driver support for USB dongle:

- Userspace application to create a hotspot
- Userspace application to serve as a DHCP server
- Configurations for both user space applications

Literature survey

We will get multiple solutions to create a Wi-Fi hotspot using BeagleBone Black. These solutions come with the following variations, depending on the distribution and selected packages:

- These solutions mostly depend on packages that are already available, or at least, there are no kernel-related customizations.
- They are Debian-based solutions. These solutions assume that packages are already available, or they provide instructions to installing precompiled binaries and configure the packages manually after installation.
- Some of these solutions use SysVinit as the upstart technique, while others use systemd.
- Some of the solutions use DHCP, while others use udhcp.

One of the common things among these solutions is that they use hostapd and so will we. We will follow the approaches used in `http://www.nathandumont.com/blog/wifi-hotspot-and-dhcp-from-a-beaglebone` and `https://fleshandmachines.wordpress.com/2012/10/04/wifi-acces-point-on-beaglebone-with-dhcp/` but more coupled with Yocto Project.

Our strategy

We will use the following packages:

- **Hostapd**, as the solutions I have seen are using it.
- **Udhcp** instead of DHCP.
- We have control over **kernel**, so we will discuss kernel configurations a bit so that you are able to enable your device.

- We will use **systemd**. Until now, we have been using SysVinit. To get a flavor of systemd, this seems promising for the future.

- We will create a recipe to copy our configurations related to the required packages **to rootfs**.

 We won't be changing the default configuration files of packages. We would rather try to create our own version so that we can refer to the original at any point in time.

Enabling kernel support

In the case of desktop distributions, we don't have to do such things. This is because these distributions have most of the options configured as modules. Whenever we attach a device, these configurations are loaded. In those cases, performance is not the highest priority, but in the case of embedded distributions, it is. To configure our kernel, let's invoke `menuconfig` using the following command line:

```
$ bitbake -c menuconfig virtual/kernel
```

This command will launch a separate terminal showing `menuconfig`. We need to modify the following two sections to configure our device.

Networking support – wireless

I have selected the following, skipping those that are not selected.

```
----Wireless
<*>     cfg80211 - wireless configuration API
[*]       enable power save by default
[*]       cfg80211 DebugFS entries
[*]       cfg80211 wireless extensions compatibility
<M>     Generic IEEE 802.11 Networking Stack (mac80211)
[*]     PID controller based rate control algorithm
-*-     Enable LED triggers
-*-     Export mac80211 internals in DebugFS
[*]     Trace all mac80211 debug messages
```

Device Drivers > Network device support > Wireless LAN > Atheros Wireless Cards

To avoid a long listing, I will show you only the selected ones. For your device, this will be different. We are using the carl9170 community Linux driver.

```
--- Atheros Wireless Cards
<M>    Atheros 5xxx wireless cards support
-*-    Atheros 5xxx PCI bus support
<M>    Atheros 802.11n wireless cards support
[*]      Atheros ath9k PCI/PCIe bus support
[*]      Atheros ath9k AHB bus support
[*]      Atheros ath9k rate control
<M>    Atheros HTC based wireless cards support
<M>    Linux Community AR9170 802.11n USB support
[*]      SoftLED Support
[*]      DebugFS Support
<M>    Atheros 802.11ac wireless cards support
```

 Kindly note that there are different sets of configurations available for various sets of devices. So, you may need to choose different configurations for your device.

A better approach toward Kernel configurations

The method of configuration using menuconfig is easy to use while experimenting. However, once we know the exact delta of configurations required to enable a device, we should use this information and create a file ending in the .cfg extension. For example, we will call it zexel.cfg and place the following contents in it:

```
CONFIG_ATH_COMMON=m
CONFIG_ATH_CARDS=m
CONFIG_CARL9170=m
CONFIG_CARL9170_LEDS=y
CONFIG_CARL9170_DEBUGFS=y
CONFIG_CARL9170_WPC=y
```

Now, perform the following steps

1. Create a Linux directory under `meta-ybdevelop/recipes-*/`.

2. Place this configuration file in the files directory in the path mentioned in *Step 1*.

3. Create a `bbappend` file for our kernel, and add a path to the configuration file using the `SRC_URI_append` syntax.

4. Set the `FILESEXTRAPATH` variable so that these `.cfg` files are added to the lookup path.

This way, our configurations will be automatically applied to the kernel version we are using. We don't have to enable them manually each time we rebuild our kernel.

 We can organize all our kernel configurations used in this chapter or the previous ones in different `.cfg` files.

Copying firmware

You can get appropriate firmware from `http://git.kernel.org/cgit/linux/kernel/git/firmware/linux-firmware.git`. To do this, you need to first clone this and then copy the appropriate firmware file to `lib/firmware` on `rootfs`. In our case, this is `carl9170-1.fw`. So, we copied it to mounted SD card's root directory in the `lib/firmware` path. If you fail to copy this, you will get an error saying firmware not found while trying to detect the USB Wi-Fi dongle.

 In most cases, you can use `poky/meta/recipes-kernle/linux-firmware_git.bb`. For `carl9170`, you need to remove firmware in the install step.

Using the previous kernel version

After having enabled kernel configurations, build a new root filesystem and boot up the target. When I booted up the target, I was able to successfully detect the ZyXEL USB dongle as the following log appeared in dmesg:

```
[   11.080312] usb 2-1: new high-speed USB device number 2 using musb-
hdrc
[   11.282092] usb 2-1: New USB device found, idVendor=0586,
idProduct=3417
[   11.289320] usb 2-1: New USB device strings: Mfr=16, Product=32,
SerialNumber=48
[   11.297257] usb 2-1: Product: ZyXEL NWD271N
```

However, when I ran iwconfig, I got the following output, which is not what I wanted:.

```
# iwconfig
wlan0     no wireless extensions.
lo        no wireless extensions.
eth0      no wireless extensions.
```

When I searched for the cause of the failure, it turned out that support for this specific kernel version 3.14.19 is broken. So, I needed to try some previous versions. Looking into recipes, I came to know of the 3.12.30 version. So, I downgraded to this version using the following line in the auto.conf file. You can use the same line in local.conf, if you are not maintaining an auto.conf file:

PREFERRED_VERSION_linux-ti-staging = "3.12.30"

Run bitbake core-image-sato again to get the images created. Prepare an SD card and boot up the target. Check whether the device is working or not. In my case, I was able to get the following output for iwconfig:

```
# iwconfig
wlan0     IEEE 802.11bgn  ESSID:off/any
          Mode:Managed Access Point: Not-Associated   Tx-Power=0 dBm
          Retry  long limit:7   RTS thr:off   Fragment thr:off
          Encryption key:off
          Power Management:off
```

This means it got detected successfully, and we are ready to move further.

Issue with rfkill

In the default kernel configuration, `CONFIG_RFKILL` is enabled, as we can see in `arch/arm/configs/omap2plus_defconfig` under kernel `${WORKDIR}`:

```
CONFIG_RFKILL=y
```

This caused Wi-Fi to block. This can be checked using the following command:

```
# rfkill list
```

It can then be unblocked using the following command:

```
# rfkill unblock all or rfkill unblock wifi
```

However, I have selected the dirty way of disabling it in kernel so that I don't have to execute these commands every time. The clean way is to keep it, and put these commands in an upstart script.

Required packages

As we have already discussed, we will use `hostapd` to turn the board into an access point. The recipe for this is available at `meta-oe/meta-oe/recipes-connectivity/`. Make sure this layer is enabled in `bblayers.conf`. Also, let's create a separate package group to enable packages to our root filesystem. Let's name it `packagegroup-yb-hotspot.bb` and add `hostap-daemon` to it:

```
RDEPENDS_${PN} = " \
        hostap-daemon \
"
```

We will add another recipe to it, but wait until we have it created. Also, this is just the difference that we are talking about. Otherwise, you will have to add other lines, such as inherit and SUMMARY and LICENSE, to it in the same way.

Changing upstart scripts

Before we start writing our recipe, we need to decide which upstart service manager type we will use. We have two options. One is SysVinit, which we were using until now. The second one is to use systemd. We will use the latter system because it is new and emerging, you should know about it, and I like it. It has a much better startup time. To enable it, we need to add the following lines to our `auto.conf` file:

```
DISTRO_FEATURES_append = " systemd"
VIRTUAL-RUNTIME_init_manager = "systemd"
DISTRO_FEATURES_BACKFILL_CONSIDERED = "sysvinit"
```

We will have to build the full image again using the usual commands.

 It is recommended that you force recompile virtual/kernel so that all the modules are also rebuilt.

I used the following command to recompile virtual/kernel:

```
$ bitbake -C compile virtual/kernel; bitbake core-image-sato
```

If you want to check systemd, it is recommended that you add `systemd-analyze` to the image by adding it to the preceding package group and play with it.

Even after having built and rebooted the images, sometimes things won't work like magic on the first go. However, lessons learned the hard way are real lessons. What have we missed here? systemd requires extra kernel configurations as well, so we need to enable CGROUPS, AUTOFS4, FANOTIFY, and DEVTMPFS:

```
General setup   --->
  [*] Control Group support   --->
File systems   --->
  [*] Filesystem wide access notification
  <*> Kernel automounter version 4 support (also supports v3)
Device Drivers   --->
Generic Driver Options   --->
    [*] Maintain a devtmpfs filesystem to mount at /dev
    [*]   Automount devtmpfs at /dev, after the kernel mounted the
    rootfs
```

I still found a crash due to CONFIG_FHANDLE still not being set, you can set it using the following:

```
General setup   --->
 [*] open by fhandle syscalls
```

This will resolve the crash. We will now be able to successfully log in to a system that is using systemd instead of SysVinit.

Recipe Hotspot-yb

When we run a `tree` command on the `hotspot-yb` recipe directory, we get the following output:

```
$  tree ../meta-ybdevelop/recipes-example/hotspot-yb/
../meta-ybdevelop/recipes-example/hotspot-yb/
├── files
│   ├── aplaunch.sh
│   ├── ap.service
│   ├── carl9170.conf
│   ├── hostapd.conf.yb
│   ├── setup-gw.sh
│   ├── udhcpd.conf.yb
│   └── udhcpd.leases
└── hotspot-yb_0.1.bb
```

First, we will discuss these files one by one, although these are mostly available through the links shared in *Literature Survey*. Yet, some files are renamed, or some of the contents are changed. We won't be discussing the contents, rather just the use of these files. Next, we will discuss our recipe, `hotspot-yb_0.1.bb`, which is also not very complex, as it has only two simple tasks.

The access point launcher script

`aplaunch.sh` is an access point launcher script. This script is triggered by `systemd daeipt`. It performs the following major tasks:

- Launches the DHCP server
- Launches the hostap daemon
- Launches the gateway setup script to set up iptables

Systemd service unit file

ap.service is the systemd service unit file. This is the simplest systemd unit file to set up our board as an access point on board bootup. Here's the content of the simple unit:

```
[Unit]
Description=WiFi Access Point

[Service]
WorkingDirectory=/lib/systemd/scripts/
ExecStart=/lib/systemd/scripts/aplaunch.sh

[Install]
WantedBy=multi-user.target
```

Configuration file for the driver module

carl9170.conf is the configuration file for driver module. There were some errors related to encryption. To avoid those, we need to disable hardware encryption. This is not relevant in all cases. It contains just this line:

```
options carl9170 nohwcrypt=1
```

Configuration file for hostapd

hostapd.conf.yb is the configuration file for hostapd.

We can find /etc/hostapd.conf, which is installed by the package installer. We don't want to overwrite it. We provide a different name for our configuration file so that we can consult the original at any time. We will use the simplest one with the following contents in it:

```
interface=wlan0
driver=nl80211
ssid=YBAP
channel=1
hw_mode=g
auth_algs=1
wpa=3
wpa_passphrase=1234567890
wpa_key_mgmt=WPA-PSK
wpa_pairwise=TKIP CCMP
rsn_pairwise=CCMP
```

The gateway setup file

`setup-gw.sh` is the gateway setup file. In some cases, it may not be required. For us, it contains the following lines:

```
#!/bin/sh
iptables --table nat --append POSTROUTING --out-interface eth0 -j
MASQUERADE
iptables --append FORWARD --in-interface wlan0 -j ACCEPT
```

The udhcp configuration file

`udhcpd.conf.yb` is the configuration file for udhcp. You can adjust it according to your requirements. We have kept this file for a generic case. The location of this configuration file is `/etc/dhcpd.conf`:

```
start 192.168.11.64
end 192.168.11.79
interface wlan0
max_leases 10
option subnet 255.255.255.0
```

The udhcp empty lease file

This is just an empty file named `udhcpd.leases`, required by udhcpd to keep the leases. It will be created under the `/var/lib/misc` directory in the root filesystem of the target.

Recipe file hotspot-yb_0.1.bb

Let's go through the sections one by one:

- The first most important thing is the use of `systemd` class in line number 6:

  ```
  inherit systemd
  ```

- Next, we set variables related to this class. In the first set of variables, we set the name of our service. In the next set, we enable this service:

  ```
  SYSTEMD_SERVICE_${PN} = "ap.service"
  ```

- The list of configuration files is maintained using the SRC_URI variable:

  ```
  SRC_URI = " \
    file://ap.service \
    file://aplaunch.sh \
    file://hostapd.conf.yb \
  ```

```
file://udhcpd.conf.yb \
file://udhcpd.leases \
file://carl9170.conf \
file://setup-gw.sh \
"
```

- We have the list of files to be installed. We now need to install them. Kindly note the destination directories:

```
install -d ${D}${sysconfdir}

install -m 644 ${WORKDIR}/hostapd.conf.yb ${D}${sysconfdir}

install -m 644 ${WORKDIR}/udhcpd.conf.yb ${D}${sysconfdir}

install -m 644 ${WORKDIR}/carl9170.conf ${D}${sysconfdir}/
modprobe.d/

install -d ${D}${OPKGLIBDIR}/misc/

install -m 644 ${WORKDIR}/udhcpd.leases ${D}${OPKGLIBDIR}/misc/

install -d ${D}${systemd_unitdir}/scripts

install -m 755 ${WORKDIR}/aplaunch.sh ${D}${systemd_unitdir}/
scripts/

install -m 755 ${WORKDIR}/setup-gw.sh ${D}${systemd_unitdir}/
scripts/

install -d ${D}${systemd_unitdir}/system

install -m 644 ${WORKDIR}/ap.service ${D}${systemd_unitdir}/
system/
```

- Finally, we will tell the packaging tasks what files need to be packaged:

```
FILES_${PN} += "${systemd_unitdir}/scripts ${sysconfdir}
${OPKGLIBDIR}"
```

Enabling hotspot-yb

To enable hotspot-yb, add it to packagegroup-yb-hotspot.bb, as shown here:

```
RDEPENDS_${PN} = " \
       hostap-daemon \
       hotspot-yb \
"
```

Managing in packagegroups

I have broken up all of the artifacts into the following three package groups:

- `packagegroup-yb-develop.bb`
- `packagegroup-yb-hotspot.bb`
- `packagegroup-yb-surveillance.bb`

We can use all these package groups simultaneously by adding all of them in the `core-image-sato.bbappend` file as follows:

```
IMAGE_INSTALL_append = " packagegroup-yb-hotspot"
  packagegroup-yb-develop \
  packagegroup-yb-surveillance \
  "
```

We may face issues if the single kernel is not working after all. I haven't tried, but I am hopeful that the camera will work for both the kernels in the same way. So, we can use 3.12.30 for both *Chapter 7, Turning BeagleBone to Home Surveillance System*, and this chapter. Give it a try!

Let's take a look at the procedure to connect with an Android mobile phone. We'll look at connecting with client devices by following these steps:

1. Boot your BBB board.
2. Ensure that the Wi-Fi dongle is enabled by this command:
   ```
   ifconfig -a
   ```
3. It should show wlan0 up.
4. Search for the BBB access point name in your client device and try connecting to it.
5. Modify the settings in your Android device from static IP to DHCP (since we are having the DHCP server running in our BBB, it will assign it for you).

Knowing the issues/enhancements

We haven't resolved all of the issues for several reasons. These reasons are as follows:

- The biggest and greatest is time.
- Most of these issues don't fall in the scope of the book. They are related to the configuration of system, or hardware (which can change for users) driver implementation, or network configurations.
- Try using ConnMan to achieve the same goal. This will be a rather simple implementation. The ConnMan package is already enabled in `core-image-sato`, but you will need `connmanctl` from the `connman-client` package, which is built in but not added to `rootfs` by default. With these packages, you can issue `connmanctl enable wifi` and `connmanctl tether wifi SSID Passphrase` and try connecting the devices.

Having said that, the following are the known issues with this implementation:

- Our service fails to start at boot time. If we check the status, it shows `Active: inactive (dead)`.
- When we connect to our device and browse, we get some data loss messages continuously, and sometimes it breaks. However, this issue is solely related to hardware, as most of the reviewers did not encounter these issues with their hardware.

Summary

In this chapter, we converted our BeagleBone Black to a Wi-Fi hotspot. To achieve this, we modified kernel configurations and created a recipe to bundle all of the configuration files. Also, we changed systemd instead of the SysVinit script.

Index

A

aplaunch.sh 101
append files 65
ap.service 102

B

BeagleBone
  auto.conf 6
  bblayers.conf 6
  booting 14
  building for 3
  build, triggering 7
  local.conf 4
  site.conf 6
BeagleBone, as Wi-Fi hotspot
  about 93
  enhancements 106
  hotspot-yb, enabling 104
  issues 106
  kernel support, enabling 95
  literature survey 94
  managing in packagegroups 105
  required packages 99
  requisites 94
  strategy 94
  upstart scripts, changing 100
  use case 93
BeagleBone Black
  hardware setup 11, 12
  serial setup 12, 13
**BeagleBone, turning into home
    surveillance system**
  about 79
  bad plugins 83

based on Debian/Angstrom 81
base plugins 82
camera-detection issues 89
client side 82, 88
enhancements 92
existing solutions 80
good plugins 83
GStreamer and plugins, enabling 83, 84
GStreamer pipeline 86
host/server side 81
implementing 82
meta-ti layer, building with 90
problem statement 79
requisites 80
selected solution 81
specialized capturing hardware,
    requisites 80
specialized software application,
    requiring 80
ugly plugins 83
UVC driver DMA issue 90
Video4Linux2, enabling 84, 85
BitBake
  about 22
  history 21
  legacy tools 22
bitbake.conf
  about 17
  architecture-dependent build variables 17
  build flags and options 18
  download locations 18
  general work, for build system 18
  output directories, for build system 18
  package default variables 17
  rootfs population information 18
  specific image creation 18

standard target filesystem paths 17
utilities 18

BitBake execution
  about 24
  metadata, parsing 24
  tasklist, preparing 25
  tasks, executing 25
BitBake options
  about 26
  alternate provider, using 27
  build, continuing even in case of errors 27
  dependency graph, generating 30
  dry run 29
  environment, obtaining 29, 30
  force-specific task 27
  level, debugging 29
  log levels 31
  parse only 29
  profile 31
  shared state, turning off 31
  specific recipe, building 26
  specific task, executing 28
  stamps, invalidating 28
  UI type, selecting 31
  verbosity, increasing 28
  versions, displaying 29
Board Support Packages (BSPs) 5
build directories, helloworld recipe
  about 39
  deploy-ipks 39
  image 39
  license-destdir 39
  package 39
  packages-split 39
  patches 39
  pkgdata 39
  pseudo 39
  sysroot-destdir 39
  temp 39

C

carl9170.conf 102
classes directory 64
compile tasks
  debugging 73, 74
configuration files

about 15
  bitbake.conf 17
  machine.conf 15-17
constituent variables
  BASE_WORKDIR 38
  EXTENDPE 38
  MULTIMACH_TARGET_SYS 38
  PN 38
  PR 38
  PV 38
  TMPDIR 38
contents, helloworld recipe
  about 36
  DESCRIPTION 36
  do_compile 37
  do_install 37
  LICENSE 36
  LIC_FILES_CHKSUM 36
  PR 36
  S 37
  SECTION 36
  SRC_URI 36
contents, of layers
  about 60
  classes directory 64
  conf directory 60-63
  COPYING.mit 64
  README file 64
  recipes-* directory 63
COPYING.mit 64

D

DESCRIPTION element 70
do_clean + function 42
do_cleansstate + function 43

E

eMMC (embedded MultiMediaCard) 14

G

gaku
  about 45
  recipe 46
GStreamer pipeline 86, 87
GStreamer recipes, short trip

about 51
action time 55
ALLOW_EMPTY 53
conditional overriding mechanisms 54
EXTRA_OECONF 53
FILESPATH 54
FILES_ variables 53
same code, reusing 55
same code, sharing 55
variable assignments, types 52
Variable Flags 53
GStreamer tool
about 84
Element Flags section 84
Element Properties section 84
Factory Details section 84
Plugin Details section 84

H

hardware setup, BeagleBone Black 11, 12
helloworld deployment
about 43
image, making dependent on package 44
package, installing manually 43
helloworld recipe
build directories 39
contents 36
creating 33-37
deploying 43
naming and related variables 37
tasks 40
hostapd.conf.yb 102
host environment, Yocto Project
ADT Installer Extras 3
documentation 2
essentials 2
graphics 2
setting up 1, 2
hotspot-yb recipe
about 101
access point launcher script 101
carl9170.conf 102
hostapd.conf.yb 102
recipe file hotspot-yb_0.1.bb 103, 104
setup-gw.sh 103
systemd service unit file 102

udhcpd.conf.yb 103

K

kernel support, enabling
about 95
Atheros Wireless Cards 96
firmware, copying 97
issue with rfkill 99
kernel configurations 96
previous kernel version, using 98
wireless networking support 95

L

layer.conf file 60-63
layers
about 57
append files 65
conditional selection, based on 64, 65
contents 60
creating, script used 57-59
packagegroups 66
legacy tools, and BitBake
build systems, coupling to 23
collaborating 23
cross-compilation 22
exploit parallelism 23
extending 23
inter-package dependencies, resolving 22
reusing 23
variety, of architecture 23
variety, of build systems distros 23
variety, of target distribution 22
libowl-av 46
LICENSE element 70
LIC_FILES_CHKSUM element 70
listtasks utility task 42

M

machine.conf 15-17
meta-ti layer
building with 90
enabling 91
fetching 91
priority, setting 91

O

OpenEmbedded 22

P

package, adding to root filesystem
  about 77
  action 78
  image bbappend 78
  packagegroup 77
package control variables
  about 46
  build dependencies (DEPENDS) 46
  PROVIDES 48
  RCONFLICTS 48
  RPROVIDES 49
  RREPLACE 48
  runtime dependencies (RDEPENDS) 47
  runtime recommendations
    (RRECOMMENDS) 47
packagegroups 66
package_write_<package> statement 42
PAC-MAN 69
Pacman4Console game
  about 69
  basic elements 70
  compile tasks, debugging 73, 74
  developing 70
  hardware requisites 69
  package contents, adding 76, 77
  S directory 72, 73
  source control 71
  task, installing 75
  work directory 72

R

README file 64
recipe, for gaku
  package control variables 46
  source control 49
recipes-* directory 63
Rtph264pay 87

S

SD card

formatting 8-10
  images, copying to 10
  partitions, creating 8-10
SECTION element 70
serial setup, BeagleBone Black 12, 13
setup-gw.sh 103
source control, in gaku recipe
  about 49
  classes, inheriting 51
  PV calculation 49
  S directory 51
  SRCREV 49
  SRC_URI specification 50

T

tasks 28
tasks, helloworld recipe
  about 40
  build 40
  clean 42
  cleanall 43
  cleansstate 42
  compile 41
  configure 41
  default tasks, overriding 43
  Devshell 42
  fetch 40
  install 42
  package 42
  patch 41
  unpack 41

U

udhcpd.conf.yb 103
Udpsink 87

V

V4l2src 87
variable assignments, types 52
Video4Linux2
  about 84
  append, using 85
  enabling 84, 85
  in-place amendment 85
  local.conf, using 85, 86

VLC 88

x264enc 87

Yocto Project
  host environment, setting up 1, 2
  obtaining 3

Thank you for buying
Using Yocto Project with BeagleBone Black

About Packt Publishing

Packt, pronounced 'packed', published its first book, *Mastering phpMyAdmin for Effective MySQL Management*, in April 2004, and subsequently continued to specialize in publishing highly focused books on specific technologies and solutions.

Our books and publications share the experiences of your fellow IT professionals in adapting and customizing today's systems, applications, and frameworks. Our solution-based books give you the knowledge and power to customize the software and technologies you're using to get the job done. Packt books are more specific and less general than the IT books you have seen in the past. Our unique business model allows us to bring you more focused information, giving you more of what you need to know, and less of what you don't.

Packt is a modern yet unique publishing company that focuses on producing quality, cutting-edge books for communities of developers, administrators, and newbies alike. For more information, please visit our website at www.packtpub.com.

About Packt Open Source

In 2010, Packt launched two new brands, Packt Open Source and Packt Enterprise, in order to continue its focus on specialization. This book is part of the Packt Open Source brand, home to books published on software built around open source licenses, and offering information to anybody from advanced developers to budding web designers. The Open Source brand also runs Packt's Open Source Royalty Scheme, by which Packt gives a royalty to each open source project about whose software a book is sold.

Writing for Packt

We welcome all inquiries from people who are interested in authoring. Book proposals should be sent to author@packtpub.com. If your book idea is still at an early stage and you would like to discuss it first before writing a formal book proposal, then please contact us; one of our commissioning editors will get in touch with you.

We're not just looking for published authors; if you have strong technical skills but no writing experience, our experienced editors can help you develop a writing career, or simply get some additional reward for your expertise.

Embedded Linux Development
with Yocto Project

ISBN: 978-1-78328-233-3   Paperback: 142 pages

Develop fascinating Linux-based projects using
the groundbreaking Yocto Project tools

1. Optimize Yocto Project's capabilities to develop
   captivating embedded Linux projects.

2. Facilitates efficient system development
   by helping you avoid known pitfalls.

3. Demonstrates concepts in a practical and
   easy-to-understand way.

Rapid BeagleBoard Prototyping
with MATLAB and Simulink

ISBN: 978-1-84969-604-3   Paperback: 152 pages

Leverage the power of BeagleBoard to develop
and deploy practical embedded projects

1. Develop and validate your own embedded
   audio/video applications rapidly with
   Beagleboard.

2. Create embedded Linux applications on a
   pure Windows PC.

3. Full of illustrations, diagrams, and tips for
   rapid Beagleboard prototyping with clear,
   step-by-step instructions and
   hands-on examples.

Please check **www.PacktPub.com** for information on our titles

Learning BeagleBone

ISBN: 978-1-78398-290-5   Paperback: 206 pages

Learn how to love and care for your BeagleBone and teach it tricks

1. Develop the practical skills that are required to create an embedded Linux system using BeagleBone.

2. Use the embedded Linux software to control LEDs on the BeagleBone, empowering you to create LED flash patterns.

3. A hands-on guide, supported by practical examples to integrate BeagleBone into your projects.

Embedded Linux Projects Using Yocto Project Cookbook

ISBN: 978-1-78439-518-6   Paperback: 324 pages

Over 70 hands-on recipes for professional embedded Linux developers to optimize and boost their Yocto know-how

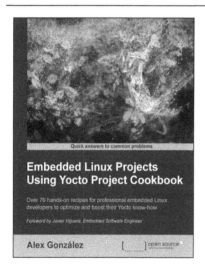

1. Explore best practices for all embedded product development stages.

2. Use what is quickly becoming the standard embedded Linux product builder framework, the Yocto Project.

3. Easy to follow guide to solve all your project woes.

Please check **www.PacktPub.com** for information on our titles